Bliss 101

A Pocket Guide for Finding Bliss and Freedom

Also by CAROLE PRISM

Book

GOING FOR MORE

Game

The Follow Your Bliss Deck

Bliss 101

✦

A Pocket Guide for Finding Bliss and Freedom

Carole Prism

iUniverse, Inc.
New York Lincoln Shanghai

Bliss 101
A Pocket Guide for Finding Bliss and Freedom

iUniverse books may be ordered through booksellers or by contacting:

iUniverse
2021 Pine Lake Road, Suite 100
Lincoln, NE 68512
www.iuniverse.com
1-800-Authors (1-800-288-4677)

ISBN: 978-0-595-45221-7 (pbk)
ISBN: 978-0-595-69404-4 (cloth)
ISBN: 978-0-595-89530-4 (ebk)

Printed in the United States of America

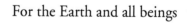

For the Earth and all beings

"Joseph Campbell said follow your bliss. We think those are the best words spoken by the human tongue."
Esther Hicks, *The Teachings of Abraham*, from the Secret DVD

Contents

Preface

It was in the fall of 2006 that I chose to make a career change and focus on writing. I had written screenplays, an inspirational book and created two growth games/decks of cards in the past and was yearning to put pen in hand again. My first thought was to rework a screenplay into a novel. Getting the words from my mind to the page was like pulling teeth. Results were stale. I gave up on the idea and retired to my inner world where I sought guidance. I prayed and stated affirmations to myself until I heard the still, small voice within me state clearly: "Write the bliss book". Being a person strongly motivated by bliss and having already created the Follow Your Bliss Deck that I used on a television show in Honolulu, I thought the idea sounded good. What moved me was that it had the ring of truth to it. I had not previously thought of creating a non-fiction book derived from the Deck. The fact that a new idea had emerged gave me energy and enthusiasm. Within hours, I was at the computer, the words flowing.

The result is the book you hold in your hands.

Acknowledgements

My deepest gratitude goes out to my daughters, Helen Zeldes-Collison and Sandy Zeldes, and to the Universe for the support, encouragement, inspiration and guidance given to me, especially for pursuing my creativity and writing.

Sandy and Helen have been excellent teachers and models for me as they live by higher goals and commit to their dreams, while maintaining integrity, innocence and purity of heart.

Introduction

It was after years and dozens of experiences of trusting the process of following my bliss and energy that I began to define the process as such. Following my energy and seeking bliss had become a pattern for me. Initially, I behaved so out of the box that my behavior made no sense to others, even to myself. I just knew I had to go, be, do what I felt was right for me, and be where my energy was flowing and my vibration was at a high level. I began to see bumper stickers on cars that said: Follow Your Bliss. Yes, I thought. That is what I am doing, what I am about.

Trusting the process led to a dramatic decision that has shaped my life and solidified my commitment to freedom, empowerment and bliss.

"What's this, you are moving where?" "You don't know what you're doing." These are examples of people's responses when I spoke of moving to Hawaii. This was a pivotal decision for me as it was based on where my energy was going and where I felt tremendous joy. This was absolutely contrary to other's feelings about the move. I stood my ground and moved to Hawaii, selling my belongings and venturing to what was comparable to a third world country and doing so alone. I had visited Hawaii previous to the move and had felt what I called "Paradise Consciousness" while in the islands. Paradise consciousness was a state of being carefree, unattached, free and blissful. I had never felt the degree of openness and self-esteem as when I first visited Hawaii. There was no turning back. I had to be here and it has been good.

Since the move to Hawaii, I have been surrounded by the magic that is in the air, water and land. Hawaii has a special ability to push people higher and deeper than they have gone before. Such has been the case with my continuing interest and devotion to energy and bliss. Questions have emerged; doors have opened as others have closed. Always I ask, where is my energy going, where is my bliss?

What is bliss? How do you know when you feel it?

Here are some of my observations and experiences of bliss:

Watch a baby explore its' world with zeal, intent only on discovery, on learning. Witness new parents during their first moments with their child.

Do you treasure your freedom? Flash back to a time when you felt exhilaratingly free, carefree, in love with life.

What were your graduation days like or would you like them to be? A sense of completion and readiness for the unknown, the unfamiliar? Graduation days can emerge from out of the box experiences when you are catapulted to new insights and move beyond your current state of functioning. Completion, moving out into the unknown can be peak experiences.

Remember the feelings on your first adventure, perhaps traveling to a foreign country. The thrill of doing and seeing something new is a tremendous stimulant and causes energy to flow freely during these adventures.

Sexual intimacy. What a portal to higher consciousness sex can be! The physical sensations, the closeness with another, the love and oneness can be ecstatic. Such has been the case for me and perhaps for you.

Remember when you decided to switch careers and did so despite other's warnings of financial doom and foolishness on your part? You followed your passion, your dream down whatever pathways it led you, let go of your reservations and went for it. That was exercising your freedom, a heady mix of empowerment and excitement.

The above is a sampling of my experiences and my witnessing others on their journey to bliss. Your experience of joy and bliss may be totally different and unique. I believe that we are individuals with an infinite variety of experiences of bliss, empowerment, freedom and the free flow of energy. I am not an authority on what bliss and freedom mean to you. My goal is to be a catalyst for you to find your own truth and bliss. Bliss 101 can be the encouragement for you to look within yourself to claim your highest good.

While many others have written about this subject, there is uniqueness to this pocket guide. In the guide, you will find what I call "eracism". Eracism means erasing the boxes you have put around yourself, stopping yourself from going for your dreams. The stereotypes embedded within sexism, ageism, racism (all the isms) restrict you from validating your own power and joy. The isms are subtle and so deeply ingrained in your mind that you forget they are programs and expectations you have accepted as truth. It is good to question and review these isms, these stereotypes. Let's erase those isms, break free from the grief they cause us.

Along with the support to break free from stereotypes (see the chapter: Think Out Of The Box) is a unification of personal happiness, bliss and freedom with loving the Earth. In these two ways, my intention is to bring a fresh breeze into the whole subject area of following your bliss.

It may seem impractical, frightening, to base decisions on where your bliss is as you have been taught to go the safe route, trust security and the even tempered path. Forget being or feeling extraordinary, don't dare step out and up into your power or freedom. Knowing where your energy is and how to follow it is a courageous way to run your life.

We live in a time of global crisis, with the predominant reaction and emphasis being one of fear. What better time than today to focus on the basic truths and principles of a joyous life? Hope is the antidote to fear. Your hope resides in taking hold of the great spiritual principles that are grounded in science. It appears it is up to us, individually, to take hold of the reins of our minds and souls to move forward and create a world of peace and joy.

Shall we get started?

Carole Prism

1

Ask For Guidance

"We must come to understand what faith and prayer really are and how it is that God works through us. We must no longer believe that God is a God only of some one race or creed, for God is the God of all life, of everyone's life, of everything that lives. God is the intelligence, the beauty, the law and order, the animating principle in and through everything."
Ernest Holmes in *The Art of Life*

Guidance comes in many forms. Prayer is the most common form of seeking guidance. Metaphysical teachers agree that you should be clear about what you ask for when composing prayers. The following is an example of a prayer I have used recently:

"Mother/Father God, what form should my writing take?"

I addressed the Higher Power as Mother/Father God. During other prayers, I have addressed God as the Universe, the light, or whatever feels right for me at the time I am in prayer. God has many names. I encourage you to use what you are comfortable with.

This prayer was a dialogue with my inner source of guidance. As previously shared in the preface, I heard what I believe was the still, small voice within me that said: "Write the bliss book". When I heard the guidance to write Bliss 101, it felt right. I felt my spirit soar when I heard those words. My feelings are a solid indicator if the guidance I am receiving is for my highest good. When guidance lifts me and inspires me, it's a go.

You can talk to a friend, counselor or minister/rabbi in the hopes that in the course of the conversation, as you lay out what is on your mind, you will gain clarity and a sense of direction. Please remember to go back within yourself, consider the advice given and sort it out. You are the one who has the final and best guidance for yourself.

Have a psychic reading. I have functioned as a psychic and know the thrill of giving and receiving an excellent reading. In my opinion, the best readings are when you feel validated, have connected with the psychic and believe she has read your innermost dreams, hopes and gifts. I love when people say to me: "This is super. What you just said I was thinking about this morning. I may really want to explore that path".

Using divination tools on your own and with friends can be fun and helpful. Keep in mind that a Tarot card can mean something unique for you that may not be reflected in the guide provided or in your friends' interpretations.

One last thought on receiving guidance from the Universe in the form of a still, small voice or a clear affirmative sign that answers your question. When you hear a response from the Universe and you act on it, things usually fall into place quickly and effortlessly. It is an indication that you are in tune with our bliss.

Do an experiment and let your feelings be your compass and guide for one week. During this time, act on guidance you believe you are receiving.

2

Believe

There is a story I have heard from a number of sources. The basics are that when ships first appeared in the bay of a country centuries ago, when ships and Caucasian people were unknown, the indigenous people could not see them. They were invisible to these people. A shaman from the tribe could see these amazing ships as he was trained to see other worlds, was open to the unfamiliar, perhaps had seen the ships and the pale faced ones in visions. He went to the seashore and performed a shamanistic ritual for his people that enabled them to see the ships.

What this story means to me is that there may be unseen worlds, events, people around me that I can not see as I am not open to these sights; they are unknown and unfamiliar to me. I am closed to the possibility of the existence that there are creatures from other Planets who look strange to me, or that other dimensions are parallel to this dimension. I would need to be open to see them. They are outside my belief system. Actually, I do believe in these phenomenon yet I wonder how much I do resist and therefore can not see or experience.

What you believe forms your world.

You start where you are. When people enter twelve step recovery programs, they are encouraged to find something greater than themselves to believe in. If a person is an agnostic, he is asked to find an object from Nature, such as the tree outside their window to be their Higher Power.

A toddler's first belief in a higher power is belief in the power of their parents. As they grow, the toddler may become a child who has profound experiences of wonder and awe when playing with animals or noticing the play of light in their room. They may have imaginary playmates. If not discouraged by adults who view these experiences as signs of mental imbalance, then the child will embrace a belief in other dimensions and beings without fear.

As belief shapes your world, I encourage you to find an opening within you to explore the world of the wondrous.

There is a poster in my room from the film, Ghost. At the top of the poster is the word: BELIEVE. In the movie, Patrick Swayze is murdered and from the Afterlife, tries to save Demi Moore who is in danger. Moore and Whoopie Goldberg, who plays the reluctant medium, are initially resistant and closed to the possibility of life after death. It was their mutual opening to the idea that Swayze survives in another dimension and has vital information to communicate that saves Moore.

The art of believing is about balancing the rational mind with curiosity and wonder. If you remain closed and cynical, you will not see or experience the miracles that are around you. Have no fear as life will teach you so eventually you will believe in something higher and greater.

There is a paradox with connecting and believing in a Higher Power and surrendering to whatever you experience as God. As we are one with this Light and Power, it is external and at the same time, internal. The Power is within and without, greater than you, and you. I move between both realities, the external and internal. I experience Spirit as outside me, and then move inward to the play and movement of Spirit within me. What I am most comfortable with is believing that I am one with the Universe.

Here's an interesting exercise to help you become conscious of your belief system and its effect on your life.

Write down three core beliefs about yourself and about life. Three beliefs for each. Ask yourself how each core belief has shaped your present day reality. Be honest with yourself about what core beliefs are nurturing your path to bliss and which are blocking bliss.

After contemplating the above questions, what beliefs do you want to change, add or revise?

Happy trails as you venture onto the path of exploring belief.

3

Be One-pointed

Multitasking is pervasive in our lives, agreed upon as the new cultural consensus of how to be successful. We don't question its value. We do it. We multitask, over stimulate ourselves and thereby divide our energies. Our attention is not one hundred percent focused on one goal.

I found myself recently talking on the cell phone, parking my car, looking up a client's medical information and checking the clock in the car as I had an appointment with another client in a few minutes. After I exited the car in a rush to pick up a client's medications, I realized I had locked keys in the car. I was too scattered to attend to all those tasks.

That is the result of a few minutes of multitasking. What is the result when we have an important goal or goals in sight? Could I have finished the Honolulu Marathon talking on the cell phone, worrying about other people, checking the time as I proceeded? No, I don't think so. The Marathon took my one hundred percent attention. Absolutely.

I encourage you to choose one goal to focus on one-pointedly, so that your energy is razor sharp. The image of an archer, poised, still, intent on focusing on the target comes to mind when I think of the tool of being one-pointed. Visualize yourself as the archer, with words or images representing your dream written clearly on the target. Your energy is the arrow pointed at the target. You have to give your all, your intention, attention, control, visualization to hitting the bulls eye.

Once you set your sight on one goal, you do not allow yourself to be distracted. This, in and of itself, is worth the exercise as the discipline you bring to the effort to stay focused brings you satisfaction and generalizes to other areas of your life.

An example would be that you decide you want a serious, intimate relationship in your life. This is your priority. You are tired of dating, the games, and the casual encounters. Your soul longs for a partner, a solid relationship. Be one-pointed about your desire. A distraction would be spending time with someone who tells you they are not ready for a relationship. You will be tempted to compromise out of loneliness or fear that there is no one for you. You think: "why not spend time with this person, just for companionship?". Doing so takes energy away from your pursuit of the kind of relationship you want.

Another way I view this when I become one-pointed, is to tell myself it is time for me to be impeccable about this issue, this is a no compromise deal. Go for it (what I want, what I believe in) all the way. A level of commitment of this degree attracts what you need to reach your goal.

Try it on, see how this approach feels. It may bring you closer to your bliss. It has often been the path for me, the tool in my toolbox that makes things happen.

4

Be Silly
(Lighten Up)

Life can feel dense, heavy. You feel burdened. Being an adult is not what you expected. You may occasionally feel and think this way. So many issues in the world, in your life to think about. It's all too serious.

Being silly can come about in the midst of tremendous stress when you say or do something ridiculous that is a reaction to the stressors. My most recent ridiculous move was when I was doing crisis intervention work in the mental health field and was very stressed out after a sixty hour work week. Frantically, I realized I had to contact a client and get something arranged. I panicked. "Where is my cell phone?" I asked my supervisor. The cell phone was in my hand, pressed to my ear. My supervisor and I cracked up laughing.

While getting ready to paddle in an outrigger canoe a couple of weeks ago, one of the guys at the last minute said he couldn't find his sunglasses and began fishing around in the water for them. Others in the boat began to look in the water for them. Suddenly, the man says: "Oh, here they are." They were on his head, above his sun visor. Everyone laughed.

A moment of silliness can set off a series of funny events, revive your humor and help you remember to lighten up.

Watching my grandchild, Hana, play, make funny faces, respond to adults always from her magical inner child, I remember my inner child.

I encourage you to conjure up an image of yourself as a baby. You can use family photos of yourself as a baby. Remember that there was a time when you were free of inhibitions, behaved in very humorous ways, were a delight to behold and were intensely curious. Keep a photo of yourself as a baby, as a child or toddler nearby to recapture the magic of being newborn, or being a child. She is still inside, somewhere deep in your subconscious, waiting to be acknowledged.

Your inner child wants to play, throw her inhibitions away. Try it, you may like it. We are programmed to be "civilized", socially appropriate. What a drag. We have to lighten up and play if we want to experience bliss.

The trick here is not to make this a demand on yourself. It sounds like that as I write it, so I encourage you not to internalize an expectation or demand. You have enough of those.

What I have discovered is to allow myself to be vulnerable and spontaneous in and after those moments of something really silly happening, to let myself get into a giddy state of laughter, sometimes have a great belly laugh. My daughter, Sandy, will point out to those in attendance when I convulse in laughter: "Oh, she's going off again". Love it.

5

Create A Sacred Place

In Hawaii there are special sacred places called Heiaus, places of great beauty and sanctuary on each island. There are rock walls built around these Heiaus. In the Hawaiian culture, if someone broke a law or was threatened, if they could get within the walls of the Heiau before being killed, they would be safe, forgiven for their transgression. The transgressor would often have the opportunity to spend time with a Hawaiian healer, a Kahuna, and experience cleansing and healing. On the Big Island, the dramatic Place of Refuge, is often the place that visitors remember best due to its great walls, preserved village, and the peace that emanates from the surroundings that include lava rocks, ocean, foothills, caves. The Place of Refuge has magic.

I believe we all need a sacred space, a place that has privacy, and is our own refuge.

I had a period of months of being on the road, living in other people's spaces that taught me how to honor another's space, how to not be invasive. I learned how to honor whatever space I did have within another's home and keep a semblance of silence in it. If I did not have space, I pushed myself further inside myself to find that sacredness or took refuge outdoors in places of beauty.

When that period ended, I began nesting again. Once able to have and control my own space, I put into practice what I had learned about how to keep a space sacred, which means to keep a living space pure of heart, free from discord between people and in a higher vibration. I think of sacred spaces as being empty yet full. They are probably not filled to the brim with items, people, poisons, loud noise. They are filled with the Presence of Goodness, a pregnant space, filled with possibility.

I used to have a house rule that alcohol and meat were not allowed in my home. Today, I keep poisons out of my home and do not allow arguments to occur here. I have softened on the alcohol though I rarely drink and never at home. I do not eat meat, ask that others do not cook meat here, though if someone is staying with me and they bring in a leftover turkey sandwich, I do not freak out.

The old expression that "walls have ears" developed new meaning to me when I explored the after shocks of relationship earthquakes taking place in my space. I discovered that the residue of anger and sadness hung around for days. I choose to free myself from disharmony as much as I am able to, wherever I am.

My home is my place of refuge, especially from a world that is obsessively busy, stressful, filled with electromagnetic and microwave signals, poisons, pollution of all kinds and violence. Of course, the world offers delights, items of beauty, comfort, colors, plants, flowers, organic foods, great books, music, videos, and wonderful friends and family. I want the best the world has to offer in my sanctuary.

Recently, my daughter Helen, her husband Peter and Hana, visited me in my space. Within an hour of their arrival, almost everything that was not harmful was out of the cabinets, Hana had her clothing off, was exploring every nook and cranny of my sanctuary as only a fifteen month old can. The gathering produced a different kind of sanctuary than I was used to, though it was a sacred space indeed.

The laughter and joy of being with loved ones dramatically improves the frequency in a house.

You can consider designating one room in your home as the sacred space, build an altar, put crystals in the room, and keep it a private space for yourself. Or you and your partner could choose to create a sacred place on your property. Think about being in the space together in silence and each of you using the space alone.

What would a sacred space mean to you? Have you thought about having a home that is a clear space? I believe you can create a safe place, a home you can sleep soundly in. In such a sanctuary, your visitors will remark about the peacefulness of your house. What will it take?

Come up with your own guidelines about what will clear your space.

Serenity makes a quiet, gentle approach into your mind and heart when you are in a sacred place.

6

Dreamtime

I am looking out my bedroom window, drawn by the shape of a big cat at the top of a mesa near my home. I know it is a tiger and it knows I know it is there. I am frightened that the wild animal is close to my home and I pray that it does not come to hurt me. After watching the animal for awhile, I calm down and am able to consider its beauty. I long to be able to be closer to this wild, untamable creature. Suddenly, I notice it is talking to me in my head. Telepathically, I ask if I can visit it atop the mesa. I want to climb the mountain and be near it. The animal moves, heads down the foothills and slowly approaches me. We meet on the road halfway between my house and the mesa. The big cat tells me I am welcome to visit it and all the animals. Then I notice that there are animals walking behind us, all of them are communicating with me. I can understand them.

This dream came to me within the last year or two. I think of it as a big dream, one that altered my perceptions of myself and the world. I ruminated over the dream a long time, the images burned in my brain. It came from a deep part of me, it was in my soul. This part of me feels intimately connected to animals, especially animals in the wild. I am connected to the animal, to the wildness in myself. Since that dream, my relationship with animals has grown, I am comfortable, and as in the dream, feel that they communicate with me in some way. I would venture to say that my positive feelings about myself as an animal, untamed and untamable, have grown.

As I was writing this book, I decided to make a contribution to a tree planting project. I found a web site for American Forests and when I surfed it, discovered a special project called: Trees for Tigers. The project involves a partnership with Russian scientists to bring the Siberian tiger back from the brink of extinction. The trees planted will help rebuild the tiger's habitat. What a perfect way for me to follow up on the dream, to act on the love I felt for the tiger in my dream.

I have kept a dream diary over twenty years. It is enlightening to reread the older dreams to see where I was then and where I am now. The imagery changes as I deal with and incorporate the messages in the dreams.

Indigenous people have long held their dreams to be messages that are to be taken seriously. In some cultures, people gather around in the morning and share their dreams. The dreams inform the people what they need to accomplish, say or do during the day. I believe it would be smart and deeply rewarding if everyone cherished their dreams, honored the messages and tried living by what dreams say to us.

When my daughters were growing up, we would regularly share our dreams with each other. One day, Sandy woke up and told me about her dream about her birth. It was totally accurate, including a telepathic episode we shared after her birth that I had never shared with anyone. She said: "Here we go again". Sandy's sharing the dream was a turning point for me in my belief in reincarnation and it was a special moment for Sandy and I.

You can ask your dreams for information about a decision you need to make. Before going to sleep, focus on your choices, what you want to know. Look for clues in your dream. You may not get a clear dream image the first night, though if you persist with an attitude of appreciation for your dreams, you will eventually get a good dream story or image of where your deepest desire and intentions are.

Dreams are a gateway not only to the subconscious mind but to the minds of others. Distance, time and space have no bearing on dreams. Wisdom, truth, divinity, signs, guidance, humor, hope reside in dreamtime. Clues as to where your bliss is are spread out in your dreams. Dreams also function as a balancer of emotions. Feelings not acknowledged or expressed during the day will visit you in dreamtime.

Dreams that foretell the future are very interesting. One can often tell there is something unusually gripping about a precognitive dream, though just as often, you do not know it was a glimpse into the future until the content plays out in your material world.

Have you had a dream where a person who has passed on visits you, talks to you? The contact in the dream feels very real, critical information as well as healing transpires as you become aware that the dead are alive and well. These are precious dreams. I encourage you (especially if they are healing and reassuring in nature) to believe that you have had contact with the Afterlife.

If we enter into another state of mind or being while in dreamtime, then we are standing out of space and time, traveling to other dimensions. I think this is enough for me to honor my dreams, pay attention to them, and enjoy them. They could be our communication network with the Universe.

What do you think?

7

Earth First

The Earth is changing, morphing, healing and moving. This has become obvious to us. The Earth is always changing, as it is, as we are, energy changing form, a very dynamic process. Currently, the changes are taking the form of climate change and environmental crisis. Big time. We have co-created this phenomenon and need to look at our role in the earth changes.

Yes, here we are, living on, with and codependent on this massive, mysterious, dynamic, evolving version of Paradise. Paradise you say? Now we know Carole is, shall we say, off?

I insist that Earth is Heaven. We have turned the reality upside down, don't recognize the humongous gift this Planet is to all living things. As we see only a percentage of the visual, color range, what other wonders are we not seeing? There is so much more here to delight the eye, our senses and evoke Higher Consciousness than we realize.

If this is real, if Earth is meant to be Paradise, what does that mean for you as an individual? Can you just go outside and change the appearance of violence, greed and hate in the world beyond your door? Probably not, but you can turn your perceptions around again, this time visualizing a healed Earth. Imagine all beings enjoying and respecting Her. How can you be a part of the healing?

This is my belief, see if it feels right to you: I believe that what I do as a person to either help Earth cleanse and heal or do to hurt or prevent the Earth from her natural rhythm and healing process will be reflected in my material world. My actions toward Earth are important. Yours are important. Am I willing and able to adopt life affirming practices such as recycling, refrain from the use of poisons, give to organizations that are preserving biodiversity and wild habitats? Can I put Earth first when I consider decisions such as a car purchase?

You are witnessing an intensification of geologic and climate change, and it is awesome, these quick changes in the landscape and the chaos and even beauty that accompanies these changes. As a witness, perhaps you are to consider how lifestyle choices you make will effect the balance of life on Earth?

I can give you many examples, but I don't want this to be "preachy". The basic message here is to become aware of how you are a part of Nature, meditate on what your life would look like if you put the Earth first in your lifestyle.

As you think about the Earth being the Garden of Eden, engage in a research project to amplify your belief that our Planet was meant to be and still is a Paradise. Look through travel or other magazines for photographs of pristine and gorgeous places that inspire you. It could be Hawaii, the Amazon, Sedona, New Zealand. I am mentioning a few of the places that impress me. There are so many on each continent. Think about ancient ruins, such as the Mayan ruins in Central America, cities and the countryside of great countries in Europe, the Holy Land. Tune in to those sacred places that exist, here, now, that wake up your awe and love for the Earth.

Maybe our whole world would truly look and feel like Paradise if each of us showed our appreciation of the Earth by actively loving her every day. What if we extended this respect and life affirmative approach to all living beings?

I remember a story I read years ago about Luther Burbank, the man Burbank California was named after. The story went that Burbank was a botanist or a gardener, was building fabulous gardens where he lived. Then there was a major earthquake that caused much damage everywhere but in his nursery. Made me stop and think about why and how that could happen. Burbank was known as a lover of Nature which could have been like an insurance policy that covered him during this earth change.

8

Eat Live, Healthy Food

"If we want to rise to higher octaves, we must purify ourselves! We begin by purifying the body. We must eliminate those poisons that cause us—not just physically but also spiritually—to remain, relatively speaking, on lower levels of consciousness."

Chris Griscom in *Time is an Illusion*

It makes sense that we become, at the cellular/energetic level, what we eat. My original reasoning about becoming a semi-vegetarian (I do eat fish occasionally) was that I believed I absorbed into my body and consciousness the fear that animals felt as they were mistreated and killed. The antibiotics and other poisons that are pumped into animals to get them ready to be a food source for me ultimately make their way into my body.

The result has been that over the years, I have come to eat over fifty percent raw food, and most of it organic. I now crave salads, vegetables and fruit like I used to crave meats. It is fascinating how the body adapts.

Along with eating so much raw food, I minimize poisons in my life, in my diet, so that I usually eat food that has recently been harvested, that are maximally alive, energetically and enzymatically.

While I am not advocating a vegetarian diet for you, as there are people who thrive on different diets than I enjoy, I am suggesting you take a look at the amount of aliveness and wholesomeness of the food you eat. If you choose to eat meat, you can find meat from animals that have been humanely taken care of, and have been fed organic grasses, not shot full of antibiotics. If you consider the possibility that you become what you eat, at least energetically, then it follows that the highest level of aliveness and health of a food you take in, the more alive and vibrant you will be.

Food combining is the knowledge and art of planning a meal with ingredients that work together synergistically to increase the efficiency of your intestinal tract. There are books and articles to read about food combining. It is good to become knowledgeable about the science of food and food absorption.

I think about the times I have been under stress, even the stress of cross training for athletic events, and at those times, I have asked myself what are the foods that best suit my body's needs. I have found that eating a huge salad with many components including raw vegetables such as broccoli gives me an energy boost and helps protect me from the effects of stress and furthers my ability to recover from stress, both physical and mental.

What does food have to do with bliss?

I can't answer that from a scientific point of view, though I can hypothesize that if you load your body down with empty foods, processed foods laced with preservatives and poisons, then you are shutting down a pathway for bliss to breakthrough. You are creating increased density and possibly blockages in your energy flow when you ingest foods bogged down with poisons or negative energy. You are not experiencing or expressing self-love when you are mistreating your body. What you put into your body is your first and primary act of empowerment. You *can* control what you eat, the level of vitality in your body.

My daughter, Sandy, is a nutritionist. She says on her website to eat the change you want to see in the world. Check it out (www. blossomgreen.com).

9

Everything is Energy

Traditional Chinese cultures refer to this energy as Qi, the basic life force in the Universe. It is considered a spiritual or mystical energy. Hindus refer to the primal energy as prana, while Polynesian traditions call it mana. For centuries, human beings have sought to define, work with and honor the life force, which science has come to validate through quantum physics.

Quantum physics has taught us that beyond atoms are sub-atomic particles, then beyond that level, all is energy. Every solid item you see, including your body, is energy localized in form. This insight has tremendous importance for us, as we attempt to understand who we are, how we attract what we want.

Our energy field extends beyond our bodies, perhaps so far beyond that our energy touches and influences people, objects, thoughts, and life miles and miles, maybe light years from where we stand. You can touch the energy, the mind of another. If you have seen the DVD, The Secret, you remember how thoughts impact others, affecting the Planet and the Universe. This is graphically depicted in the movie. I heartily recommend that you see this video. It is enlightening, especially concerning this message, that everything is energy.

Let's take an example of how this insight can work for you in following your bliss.

You have identified that finding a partner is where your bliss is. You want a sexualove relationship. You can visualize connecting with the right person. In your visualization, see your energy fields touching now. You can be living across the country from each other, yet your thoughts and images of connecting with an ideal soul mate will connect you. The Universe will do its part by finding a way to bring you together.

Another way of saying this is that you are already connected to everything you want, everything you need. The Universe will respond to your frequent imagining of being with your partner by bringing him/her to you. The idea is to trust that you can not be separate from your heart's desire.

Let's reframe this to say that what you want is seeking you out at the energetic level. What you want, be it a partner, money, adventure, children or well-being, is honing in on you. A mutual attraction is occurring. You do not have to shoulder the burden of making it happen. Pushing hard to make something happen can form a block in the process.

The Star Wars films brought us the concept: The Force is With Us. The scenes where Yoda is teaching Luke Skywalker how to use the Force are etched indelibly in my mind. Could these be a fictionalized account on how to work with energy? The Force is with you and it is energy.

10

Explore Past Lives

It takes concentrated energy for us to explore our current life, our childhood and past history. Why bother with past lives? Do we actually live in other times and places?

I do not have proof for you that we are eternal beings who live before, between and after this current incarnation. I am simply a believer who has been blessed with mystical experiences that resulted in a growing interest in reincarnation. Not scientific proof, though enough for me to be a believer.

Today, I had a spontaneous experience of focusing on a man who lived and died just previous to my birth. This man, his history and legacy, was vividly recalled in my mind for many hours today. Once home, I did research on the Internet and my curiosity became stronger. I have no proof, there is not a physical similarity nor is there a perfect personality match. But as I explored this possibility, I can see that I have been fascinated by this person for most of my adult life.

Will this lead to feeling blissful? I get a rush of energy when I read about this person. I feel a sense of timelessness and eternity which certainly creates a deep feeling of faith and hope within me.

Contemplate the possibility of living forever, in one form or another. Is it conceivable to you that you have marched through many lives, aiming to fulfill a vision of a great life and nurture the gifts you have been given? There is so much possibility when you open to reincarnation.

You have heard of NDEs, I am sure. Near Death Experiences. Thousands of people have now been brought back to life after accidents, dying on the surgery table or after a variety of near-fatal illnesses. Once brought back to consciousness, people report amazingly similar stories of going through the tunnel, meeting a light being who helps them sort out their experiences and tells them they have to come back to their body. They have glimpses of the Afterlife, have feasted their eyes on pristine lands and beauty and have seen loved ones who have passed over. The evidence is extraordinary and though not without controversy, is accepted by most as proof of the existence of life after death. We could be evolving into a radically new vision of what we call death.

If this is true, or even possible, doors open. We see into another kingdom, we have new purpose and vision in our present life. We stretch our mental and spiritual muscles. And the questing begins in earnest as to who we were before, why we incarnated in this life, what we are here to learn.

Hypnosis can be used to explore past (and future!) lives. Though I have not tried hypnosis myself, I have read hypnotherapists' research into past and future lives. Exciting material. Consider embarking on the reincarnation adventure.

11

Fast From All Negativity

Fasting from the overload of negativity that is thrust at you daily will take discipline, though will be worth the effort. Take a few days that are reserved only for the positive.

Read positive books, view spiritual films, rent/buy uplifting DVDs such as The Secret. Feed your mind and soul the kind of information that will inspire you, help you move beyond the absorption in the outside world and all its reported problems.

The real news, if it were to be accurately reported, is that daily, there is heroism, courage, breakthroughs, miracles, healing, reunions, bliss, birth, love, joy, well being, beauty and hope everywhere. People are overcoming all manner of disabilities, dysfunctional and abusive histories, making peace with money and reaching out for goodness. It is happening every minute. Our culture and the media that has grown from this culture pushes bad news, horrific images and the denial of life at us. We are addicted to pain and horror. We can change this.

As you think about where your bliss is, you must focus on those events, thoughts, people and images that trigger bliss and freedom. Dwelling on the reports of wars, death and all the negatives out there will bring you down. You can take control of this inundation. You can control what you put into your mind, and what you feast your eyes on in the same way you can control what kinds of food you put into your body.

Taking the vow to attend to only the positive, the good and the beautiful will be challenged by others. There are times I am unaware of earth changes and human grief that is taking place elsewhere on the Planet. People remark to me that they can not believe that I don't know about the fire or whatever the disaster is that has occurred. I let people know I am focusing on the good news that is happening. I state that I am not attending to the mass media.

Along with the media blitz, you may also be inundated with negative energy, comments, thoughts that others who are uncomfortable, who are suffering, try to give you, share with you, and dump on you. You may be working or in a relationship with a "difficult person". There are a variety of ways I suggest you can deal with this, to protect yourself from negative interactions.

I recommend you do not initiate contact with someone who is intent on focusing on the negative in you, in himself or herself or the world, if this is possible. The time of fasting can be an opportunity to reevaluate your relationships, to make a conscious choice as to who you want in your life. If your commitment to focusing on the positive is strong and sustained, you may find that people who have been challenging drop away. You will not be in resonance with them any longer.

If you love someone who is "challenging" and choose to remain in the relationship, you can try interacting with them only when it is nourishing for you. You can visualize them being emotionally healthy and the two of you being in a mutually supportive relationship. You can pray for their peace of mind.

There may come a point in an intimate relationship when you find it appropriate and necessary to call a spade a spade. You can tell your significant other that during the process of fasting from negativity, you felt your energy level increase. You were happy and feeling good (something true along those lines). You want to maintain this higher level of functioning, therefore, you will not be engaging in the kind of negative loops you have fallen into with this person in the past. In order for the confrontation of the issue to be effective, I suggest that you begin and end with what you appreciate about this person. Even in the midst of dealing with the issue, you can be positive, encouraging and honest.

Bottom line is it will be up to you to control your thoughts, speech, your interactions, your habitual behavior of seeking out media and news. This exercise in fasting is very empowering and freeing.

12

Find Your Soul Mate

You are ready to connect with a soul partner or friend. Your dreams, feelings, and thoughts have led you to this awareness. It is time to have a soulful relationship.

If you are in this place, with this intention, I suggest you write down the qualities of soul you find in yourself you want to share and what is essential for you to look for in another. What does "soulful" mean to you? My thoughts on the nature of the human soul is that the soul and the Spirit are one. I have found that the soul is that part of us that is deep, truthful, open, and pure. The soul or Spirit within us is seeking answers to profound questions.

Being soulful does not mean one is not earthy, sexual, funny or light hearted. It may be easiest to eliminate those experiences and qualities that you know right off are not from the soul or good for your soul. Some situations that are not "soulful" are where lies predominate, where violence is a response to tension and conflict, or where hatred and prejudice prevail.

Here is an exercise that will help you gain clarity which is the first step in attracting a soul mate. Start with an eight and a half by eleven size page folded in half. On one side, write the heading "yes", the other side write "no". Write down every quality, experience, strength and skill you want your partner to have. The same with what you do not want. Generate a complete list on each side of the page, without censoring yourself. Next, go back over the lists to prioritize what is number one, number two, and number three. After rank ordering your lists, highlight or circle numbers one through three.

As you become clear and have a mental image through visualization of the kind of relationship you seek, bring it clearer into focus and closer to you by creating a treasure map. The map is a composite picture of what you want and can include any number of words, pictures, drawings. Include lifestyle images, words, and phrases on your map. In a treasure map I once created, I had the exact image of two hands touching with their wedding bands on. After I met the right man, this image emerged into reality, almost exactly as the magazine photos portrayed.

In order to attract the ideal partner or lover or friend into your life, you must be willing to say no to people who approach you for a relationship that is too casual, that does not offer you what you want. Saying no and being honest with the prospective partner is essential to getting to yes with the right person.

There are many web sites where you can search through the databases for profiles of people who may be looking for a soulful relationship. Try harmony.com, and match.com. I have known two women quite well who met their husbands via the Internet.

Personal ads are another means to broadcast out to the Universe what you are looking for.

The most important task for you is within yourself, the process of being honest with yourself about what you are ready for, what you want and what you will no longer accept in a relationship. The inner truth and clarity of your vision of a soul mate relationship will attract the person to you.

Be the kind of person you want to attract, and develop, and exhibit the qualities of soul that you look for in others. Like attracts like. If you want a person who is on a spiritual path, find a path or practice that works for you. If you seek a person who is drug and alcohol free, then you become drug and alcohol free.

Margaret Cho, the comedian, has said that she realized she became the person she was looking for. You can too.

13

Gratitude

If you are like me and millions of others, you are encouraged daily by other people, by media, by billboards to want what you currently do not have. Seems like everything around you is saying "buy me", "you can't live without this", feeding feelings of lack and discontent with the now of your life. While accumulating wealth is wonderful, the first step to riches is appreciating what you have and are right now, this very minute.

I finished the Honolulu Marathon a few times. One time, I had a vision of doing the whole marathon in a state of appreciation of life, of God and Nature. I dedicated every step to goodness; I appreciated every moment of the event, even the tough parts. While heading up Diamond Head, surrounded by a sea of 30,000 people, as I was saying a prayer and affirmation in my mind, I looked down to see my foot land on a twenty dollar bill. No one else seemed to notice it. It had my name on it. I believe the energy that the money represented was of gratitude and oneness with life. It was feedback from the Universe that my gratitude was received and reciprocated.

As we bless and appreciate everything that comes our way, we open the door for good and joy.

Do an experiment for one day and see your life and yourself through the eyes of appreciation, thank God for what you have, for your strengths, even your limitations. As you bless the food in your pantry, you are opening the way for more supply to be attracted to you. As you thank the Universe for the penny you find in the street, you are humbly recognizing that everything comes from the same Source. You are thanking the Source for its presence in your life. Try it for one day and see what happens.

Keep a gratitude journal, making notations in it often. You will be amazed at the blessings that have come into your life through grace. In the chaos of your fast paced life, I bet you often do not notice the great good that comes your way. The smallest blessing, once recognized, can bring you inner peace and hope.

Remember to appreciate all of yourself, the people in your life, the opportunities (even those you don't choose to act on), the delights of Nature and art.

I am grateful you bought this book. I am blessed by your reading these words and taking in what is right for you and letting go of what doesn't resonate with you.

In this moment, I hope you are pondering what you are grateful for today. We are now united through gratitude.

14

Help Someone Else

In times of stress, when you are in need, consider lending a hand to someone else. Likewise, when you are feeling peaceful, not in need yourself, ponder how you can reach out to others from the vantage point of feeling complete.

One Christmas, I was particularly lonely. I chose to spend Christmas volunteering at a religious center, cooking and serving the Holiday meal to the needy in my community. I started off the day feeling depressed, midway through serving hungry and lonely people a fabulous meal, I realized I felt content, at peace deep down inside myself.

When we are hurting, we are self-involved. In these moments of distress, we can step out of ourselves and reach out to someone else. In the process of attending to someone else's feelings and needs, we can disengage from our own suffering.

When we are calm and happy, we will often look for ways to engage others that are helpful to them, to help them reach the level of satisfaction we are feeling. I tend to look for concrete ways such as helping someone move, cook a meal for a lonely friend, drive a friend home when they don't have a car, give away an inspirational book or excess food grown in a garden.

Being a good listener when another needs to talk can be just the healing balm required for the other to move beyond their dilemma. While this may not seem concrete, it is extraordinarily helpful, as you yourself can attest to, remembering the times others have quietly and attentively listened as you have aired your thoughts, feelings and options.

Share what you know about feeling good, finding and living your bliss with others. A simple reminder to others about making the choice to feel good, to look at the positive, beyond current appearances into the true state of their being and the world, which is perfection and beauty, can be inspirational and empowering to both of you. Sharing and teaching others what you are learning about being a courageous pioneer on the path of following your bliss reinforces your path. This concept holds true as well when focusing on wealth. Help others become prosperous. Teach what you have learned about money and attracting wealth.

When deciding you want to intervene in another's life to assist them, give thought to how you can best do this in a way that will help them find strength within, find the answers to their challenges. Here's how I combined giving concrete help plus hopefully useful thoughts and ideas. A homeless woman in my community asked if she could take a shower at my home. I said yes. After she showered and we were talking, I redirected the conversation to prosperity consciousness and what I was learning about manifesting. She and I explored how she could help herself find a home by using positive techniques such as visualization.

15

Inner Divinity

Those two words say so much. It seems they are self-explanatory, yet it is a message, a reality to be explored fully.

As you can tell from this book, I believe life is an inside job. Every step along the way, one is challenged to look within, to find one's own truth. As we focus internally, we are then challenged to find the light within.

After hearing about the light within me for years, I grew weary of searching for it. Once I began visualizing a candle light, burning bright and eternally in my core, I began to get the picture.

What I got from this exercise on inner knowing is that our cells emanate a radiation, a light that enlivens and brightens everything it touches. This radiance pays no attention to the skin barrier. It easily passes through (and rejuvenates while it does), our skin and reaches other people, animals, plants, trees, everything.

The question naturally arises, where does this radiance come from? Is it in our DNA? Is it with us in the womb or does the light turn on at birth? Is it Spirit?

That is the question, right? Is the light within you your divinity? Your soul?

I think it is. How it got there, I am not sure.

Experiment with a visualization of your inner divinity. I have asked others to draw themselves with their inner divinity incorporated into the picture. The variety of visions of one's inner light is unlimited. The visualization I used is only one of unlimited possibilities in combining your creativity (drawing, writing, painting, sculpture, etc.) with your image of your inner divine self.

Try hanging your artwork in your bedroom where you can see it and meditate on the image while relaxing in bed.

This is a key to higher frequencies, bliss and joy. Knowing you are a divine being, suffused with divine energies, opens gateways to serenity. These energies must surely be regenerative and healing.

I went to the beauty pallor today, the day I edited this chapter. The woman who has been doing my hair for years initiated a wonderful conversation about Spirit. Her religious beliefs are Christian. She shared with me about her faith in God, Christ and the Holy Spirit. We moved into an engrossing discussion about the body housing the Spirit and how she has experienced her spiritual being looking out at the world through her eyes. I hadn't realized that my hairdresser and I had similar spiritual beliefs as I had known she had traditional, perhaps fundamentalist views and I am not religious. When we talked deeply about the Spirit within, about the body being a vehicle for Spirit, I understood that she and I were talking about the divinity within. Her eyes shone as we spoke in awe of the eyes being the window to the soul.

The sharing of our common ground and beliefs about the inner being that is Spirit was illuminating and reminded me that people from every walk of life and a variety of religious faiths have a common touchstone which is having experiences of the lighthouse, the divinity within. This may one of our links to each other, an insight that could lead to a rapprochement between people of different cultures and religions.

16

It's All Good

The first time I heard "it's all good", I intuited the truth of the phrase.

The context I heard it's all good in was from a personnel director of a large project who was referring to issues that involved employees, some of them rather serious and heavy. After chatting about conflict resolution, personal growth and his goals in his job as a director, he said: "It's all good". I got it. It was all good.

Translate that into your life. Consider a challenge you are dealing with, a difficult person you are involved with, a forced change in jobs, or a perceived failure or disappointment. Tell yourself that this has come into your life to bless you. You may not believe this initially. Continue the affirmation and look for the blessing, the gift. It is there. Always. It may take time for you to acknowledge or experience the gift. Nonetheless, it is there.

I have read speculation as to what the meaning is of global and cultural tragedies. In situations where many suffer, it feels sacrilegious to suggest that there is good in the midst of the crises. The situation that I have pondered is what good has come out of the Tibetans being denied their right to believe and worship God in their own way, in their own homeland and the exodus of the Dali Lama from Tibet that has resulted from oppression. When I ask others this question, everyone has replied with the same insight: the exile has brought the Dali Lama out of Tibet into the world, especially the Western World and has dispersed the Tibetans, likely the most spiritually evolved people on the Planet, into other countries. We are blessed with contact with the Dali Lama. His humor, compassion and wisdom are available to the whole world and is an inspiration and a model to us of an evolved soul.

I was once fired from a temp job. The employment company felt so bad that they had referred me to a position I did not have the skills for that they said they were going to make it up to me by sending me on an assignment to their favorite client. This led to my employment in a fabulous project that involved overseas work and contact with unusual and intelligent people, including the personnel director I referred to above. It was all good. The good initially was hidden from view due to my embarrassment at failing at an assignment and was shown the light of day very quickly when I was assigned to the fabulous job.

It may be that the environmental crisis we are currently in will be the pressure, the catalyst for a shift to a harmonious way of living that honors Nature and each other. We have to evolve emotionally, spiritually and technologically beyond where we are and this is a good thing.

If a situation is causing you fear and distress, you may be saying to yourself that this can't be good. Keep looking until you find at least one positive that has come from the negative situation you are in. Build on the positive viewpoint. You will find the gem of the blessing or it will find you.

17

Leave Everything Behind

A time of radical openness and change may come upon you and take you by surprise. Nothing feels quite right, what worked for you in business and relationships no longer works nor are any areas of your life satisfying. You may try to remedy the situation by taking a number of actions, such as changing the feng shui of your home, changing jobs though staying in the same career path, buying new clothing. Nothing seems to be helping. Relationships may be falling apart or away. There could a drastic event, perhaps even a catastrophic event such as a flood or fire and you lose everything.

Radical openness means to me that because I am either at a dead end or a phase of my life has been completed, I must approach the present and future with a level of trust that is beyond where I have been before. Once facing the possibility of leaving everything behind, I can proceed with an expanded sense of openness. It is the time of starting over, getting a second, third, fourth chance. This may go on forever. One door closing and another opening, opening up to new vistas.

Traveling is a time of being open, often radically, leaving everything behind for awhile. Being in new cultures, hearing and needing to speak in foreign languages, eating unfamiliar foods, seeing exotic and sacred places pries open the mind. We normally go about our days with tunnel vision, only seeing what is right in front of us and planning the next task. We don't look around much or look for novelty in our daily lives. We sink into routines. Married to our lifestyle, working for security, we exhaust possibilities. If you have a yen to travel, do so. Expose yourself to the unusual. If you can approach a trip with openness, you may find yourself feeling like a new person or recognizing a part of yourself that has been dormant or forgotten.

Resisting leaving everything behind can result in stagnation and frustration. We are afraid to sell our stuff, try a new locale or vocation. Our energies have become embedded in our belongings. To look at this from the Eastern point of view, our attachment to material possessions has come to control and own us. If you do sell most of your belongings, you will likely find a freeing up of your energies, enthusiasm and optimism bubbling up from the wellspring of your soul. Your bliss can now beckon you. It could be that your bliss is in a totally other life, in a new, regenerated you.

The challenging part of leaving everything behind is coming to the realization that this is what you want and need to do. It won't be comfortable when you begin to unload belongings and relationships.

This is a process that requires you to be gentle with yourself. You will be similar to the Phoenix, dying in the metaphorical fire and rising anew from your ashes. Another image that can be a positive catalyst for you in the process of starting over is that of the sculptor, chipping and cutting away at what does not fit the vision she sees in the core of the clay or stone.

You are the sculptor, the vision or art you want to create is your highest ideal, your dream. This dream is living patiently inside of you, waiting for you to give it shape by fearlessly chiseling away anything that is not true to it. Use the image of being a sculptor to hone in on your goals. As you visualize, you will gain clarity on what you have to chisel away (leave behind).

Once the vision has emerged in your mind, you can take further steps to birth it into reality.

18

Let Go

This is the companion to leave everything behind.

Learning how to release others, things, expectations, businesses, goals, low self-esteem, stress, resentments is an art and a skill we develop throughout our lives. It does not seem to come naturally to us to let go of someone we love. Oh yeah, like, okay, my partner has a drinking problem, I know he can stop drinking, I keep trying to help him stop drinking, but now, the relationship is toxic to me. Okay, I'll just let him know tonight that it is over, I have let go of him, good-bye, hasta la vista baby.

If only letting go were that linear and easy. The first step may be in letting go of the inclination to fix others to make ourselves happy.

Once you are at the point of readiness, when you have withdrawn your energy from the object or person, letting go will happen organically, naturally.

Let's check out an example of letting go of a belief that is not serving you. The belief is in scarcity and limitation. You have been programmed to believe that there is only so much money in the world, that you have to compete for supply. Years go by and you struggle with the appearance of lack. After years of study and education, you reach a mental acceptance of the new paradigm, that there is unlimited abundance in the Universe. It is available to you. Next, your mental insight will trickle down to your emotions. You will find yourself being less reactive if something pushes your scarcity buttons. It may have taken a number of strategies to move beyond your old beliefs, such as prayer, visualization, stating affirmations, study and questioning, journal writing, artwork and inspirational experiences of abundance for you to let go.

Letting go is a skill developed once you realize that holding on to people, things, negative thoughts, expectations of others only creates pain. Releasing what is not in resonance with your highest good, with your soul and your bliss will create space for what you do want to approach you. Lighten your load, especially emotionally.

A beneficial exercise is to go through every closet and drawer in your house and put aside what you have not used or worn in six months. Have a garage sale for the items that are not useful to you now or give them away. Keep only what you love and will use in your current life. You may experience grief letting go of things you have invested with your memories or identity. Thank these possessions for bringing you pleasure and gently hand them over to a person who can use them.

I do this once or twice a year. It feels like a purging. Everything seems to open up in the house, there is increased space. I feel relieved not having to take care of something that I do not need.

This morning, before one of my last edits of this manuscript, I was feeling discouraged and impatient about not seeing the result of weeks of prayer and spiritual mind treatment about increasing my cash flow. I recognized that I had done the necessary inner work to change my thinking and belief systems. I was out of "energy" to *do* anything further. I surrendered. I let go saying a prayer to the Universe and said: "It is in your hands God." When I arrived home, there was a phone call from a person who wanted to buy books and magazines from me and an email about another possibility that would be a demonstration of another wish of mine coming true. The Universe responded as I truly let go.

The sculptor does not hold on to the shavings of clay that have been cut away to reveal the masterpiece he is creating. You as the sculptor do not hold on to the aspects of your life that no longer fit your inner vision of an ideal you, an ideal life. Your inner vision is already in existence at some level; it is up to you to let go and let it breathe.

19

Like Attracts Like

"To think health when surrounded by the appearances of disease or to think riches when in the midst of the appearances of poverty requires power, but whoever acquires this power becomes a master mind. That person can conquer fate and can have what he wants"
Wallace D. Wattles in *The Science of Getting Rich*

Consider your health. If you are experiencing physical symptoms that have continued and are now, in your way of thinking, resulting in "illness", think about what you talk about. Do you talk to people about the "illness", focus on it with fear, engage with people who think and talk negatively about themselves and life? If the predominate theme of your thoughts and speech are about illness, you are maintaining this imbalance in your body. To reverse this process, experiment with thinking about health, talk about your body's ability to heal itself, frequent health food stores and see the abundance of remedies and healthy foods available. Read books about people who have healed of illnesses. You will be resonating with well being and will manifest health.

A good example of how like attracts like is when you are seeking a relationship, you get clear what you want, the qualities and values you want the woman or man to have. I have suggested previously that you develop these qualities within yourself. If you seek a person who is honest, be honest in your dealings with others. You say you want a partner who is politically active, become politically active yourself. You are looking for a person in a twelve step program and who is sober? You know the drill. I suggest you attend AA meetings and be sober. Like attracts like.

If everything is energy (which it is), you want to think about what level of consciousness/energy you live at. You wish to manifest prosperity. What energy is prosperity? How can you be at the same vibrational level as prosperity? Be in resonance with what you want. The New Roget's Thesaurus defines resonance as: "vibration, reverberation, reflection and echo". Other words that are referred to are: "melody, loudness, repetition, and sound". The words that strike me as meaningful to our understanding of resonance in the context of the law of attraction (which is what we are talking about here) are melody, reflection, echo. What is the music behind your words, your thoughts? Are you sending out the vibration/sound of prosperity? What echo can you expect to generate in the Universe?

If our words, thoughts, inner feelings, values and behavior are of deprivation, scarcity and fear, we are predominately sending out the vibration of limitation and that is the echo we will hear. That is what we will attract.

Here is a story of like attracts like. I knew a person who liked to read a magazine that was titled "Trash". I saw these magazines around the person's house one day and shortly after that, the person's front lawn was a mess. Someone had thrown trash all over the front yard!

On the positive side of the law of attraction, over a year ago, I had been reading Wallace Wattle's *The Science of Getting Rich*. I was focusing on the idea of living from the creative level not competitive level. I was thinking about my non-competitive nature, my enjoyment of working collaboratively with others. Two events occurred while I was studying SOGR. I was sitting at a bus stop at a busy shopping center musing about Wattle's principles and concepts when suddenly I saw a wad of bills on the road a few feet from me. Cars were driving by and over the money. The wind did not blow it away nor did the person sitting next to me on the bus stop bench see the bills. I picked up the money thanking the Universe for the gift. Within a few months, I attracted a professional position in the field of mental health that was based on a team approach. This position enabled me to function from the creative, cooperative level in just the manner that I had been contemplating while reading the SOGR material. In addition, the pay was at the level I had been visualizing.

Like attracts like. Study this basic principle of life and apply it to attract what you need to live your wildest and highest dreams.

20

List 10 of Your Positive Attributes

Self-esteem is a word that brings to mind what we like and do not like about ourselves. Positive self-regard, self-love, self-image refer to that aspect of ourselves that has a bad rep these days: ego or personality. In my experience as a psychotherapist, I have found that people with awareness of their strengths and an ability to call upon these inner resources are most likely to succeed in counseling and life. If you experience self-doubt, insecurities, self-hate, shame and guilt to the point that you are holding yourself back, you can do something about it. You can up level your self-awareness, increase your positive self-regard. Having a strong ego is a good thing.

Write down ten of your positive attributes, those qualities and skills that you know you possess and value. Include in the exercise those qualities that others may not like about you though you value these characteristics. A case in point is that I value my honesty and straightforward nature. Others may appreciate and acknowledge the honesty, though will complain about my ability to be assertive and speak the truth as I see it. This quality can be a plus for me all the time and can cause ripples in otherwise smooth relationships. I put that quality high on my list due to the value I place on honesty.

Your list should include little known qualities or abilities, perhaps dormant abilities, values you have though are currently not using or expressing. The importance of being honest with yourself and being able to articulate these positive aspects of yourself will become apparent after doing this exercise every few months.

Societal expectations, other's judgments may influence you when you contemplate what you truly appreciate about yourself. You may not measure up to what your parents expected, your passions may lie in creative endeavors and values that are on a path you are not on at the present time. This exercise may highlight for you how you have conformed and stopped being true to your innermost self. It's all good! You now have the deepest truth of who you are and can act from that inner truth.

I have been listing my positive attributes for over ten years at irregular intervals, usually when I become aware that my self-esteem has taken a nose dive. The top few attributes I list have remained steady over the years, with additions and subtractions further down the list. With the use of this tool, I can remind myself of the strengths I possess, especially those that have remained consistent. This is how I can validate myself, raise my self-esteem.

If you have been in therapy, you probably realize that one of the aims of therapy is to assist you in becoming your own parent or therapist. This exercise came to my mind to incorporate into my life and my work with others as an empowerment tool to stimulate growth along those lines.

21

Listen To Your Body

Your body is a million year old healer. It has developed over the eons the ability to heal itself from a vast number of symptoms, probably all if we expanded our minds to consider the possibility of limitless healing.

Over the years, I have learned to interpret the symptoms the body manifests as metaphors, messages about what one needs. The magic lies in hearing the message and giving yourself what you need, then the symptoms disappear. It is not required any longer to give you the information you need to heal.

You know the old expression that "someone is a pain in the neck"? Let's say you have pain, stiffness in your neck. Is this associated with the difficult encounter you had with a family member yesterday? I am not meaning that this person is or should be labeled as a "pain in the neck". I am suggesting you look to your experience to explain why you are in pain, look to your feelings. If your pain in the neck is related to the family member, ask yourself what you want from or with this person. The next step is to initiate a healing encounter with the person or make a new decision about how to handle the behavior that creates pain for you.

If I have a stomach ache, I will ask myself what did I "swallow" during the day that is not sitting right with me. I am not referring to food, though this could be the simplest explanation. I could have digested another's remarks that I experienced as cutting or unnecessarily critical.

My favorite example of dealing with the body this way came about during the first few weeks of an intense mental health position I held. The staff rotated being on call 24/7 from the hours of 4:30 pm to 8:00 am. The cell phone had to be on and I had to be in an area where I could get a signal. That left out hiking or swimming. I was not keen on being on call and had reservations about my ability to deal with the limitations and stress the responsibilities entailed. As the first day of being on call dawned, I woke up without a voice. Laryngitis took charge and made it impossible for me to fulfill my responsibilities. Within two days of dealing with my resistance and anxiety, my voice returned and I was able to be on call.

The body is wise beyond imagining. I sense that our cells are intelligent, that we know deep down inside what is "eating us", what causes our ailments. Trusting that we have the ability to heal ourselves is a great boon to self-confidence and inner peace. When you grasp what this means and begin looking at "illness" differently, your fear of physical ailments and pain will diminish. You can look anew at your body, not seeing symptoms as the enemy and not having to fight them. You can see that they are friends, coming to help you reach a higher level of functioning. Cooperate with your body.

Science of Mind, one of my favorite spiritual teachings, emphasizes that we are physically perfect, that "illness" is an appearance and healing takes place when we focus on the greater truth of our innate health and wholeness.

I am not suggesting that you do not seek medical help. If you choose to consult with a physician, I encourage you to continue exploring within yourself what the physical symptom is communicating.

Listening within is another tool to discover what you need, what your dreams are. Listening within and listening to your body are incredibly powerful. You will find it will take a determination on your part to create the time and space to reflect upon what you are experiencing and hearing within. It is almost impossible to hear the "still, small voice" within if you are constantly busy, around other people and responding to external demands.

Taking time out to reflect, to listen within, to hear what your body and mind are communicating is critical to the path of finding your bliss, of becoming empowered and being your own person. You are a marvel, with a treasure chest of tools and information you need to chart your own course and the treasure is found within.

22

Money Is Your Friend (The Universe is Here to Support You)

I did a psychic reading for a woman who was concerned about the possibility of repercussions of a financial decision she had made. She was fearful that she could lose all she had. During the reading, I psychically saw that if her intentions were positive and her decision did not harm anyone, then the Universe would support her. Further, I told her that the Universe is supportive of us, that we live in a loving Universe. She listened intently, taking the words in and became calm. Nothing negative has happened to her finances and she has remained financially prosperous. She has reminded me of what I said during subsequent readings.

The realization that the Universe will support our intentions was a catalyst for me to explore money in a similar vein. I have come to view money as a friend, perhaps my best friend who wants me to thrive.

You may have been brought up to believe that money is bad, the source of all evil, that wealth is meant for only a handful of people who get their riches from profiting off of our labor. While there are wealthy people who are greedy, negative, and wasteful, there are also people with little money or resources who are equally negative. Certainly, many criminals are in this lot. You can find wonderful, creative, humanitarian and cooperative rich people who have come to understand that the Universe is friendly to their aims. These folks use their money and oftentimes their fame or celebrity in marvelous ways to benefit the Planet and all of us.

I believe there will be a day when we have evolved in consciousness to the place where poverty will be looked at as unbelievable. The human race will look back at this period of time as the dark ages.

We live in a world of plenty. Abundance can be seen everywhere, especially in Nature. Our resources, even money, come from Nature. Food, dollar bills, diamonds, gold, resources of all kinds are birthed from the abundance of Nature.

Remember that everything is energy. The energy of money is like all energy. Once we have focused on its evolution from energy to matter in the form of resources, money becomes similar to manifesting apples, herbs, plants, linen, and even babies. All come from the same original substance.

While writing this chapter, I went online to research the amount of lumber and wood it takes to create paper money as this was a concern of mine. Being an environmentalist, I wanted to contribute money to replant trees that were used to create cash money. During the research, I discovered to my surprise, that paper currency is manufactured from a blend of cotton and linen fibers! Truly then, money is first energy, then moves through the form of plant life to become the cash in your pocket.

You have a choice as to how you view the world. Is this truly a world of scarcity, of lack and limitation? Is your paranoia telling you that the Universe will deprive or punish you and if so, ask yourself if this is real? Can the Higher Power (the Universe or energy) that created humans, animals, raindrops, flowers, coal/diamonds, the wind, and ocean be a limited or punishing being or phenomenon?

Wealth is a state of consciousness. We must attain a consciousness of wealth to demonstrate wealth externally. Excellent affirmations to use to develop wealth consciousness are: "I am wealth", "I am one with the Universe and the Universe is the source of immense and unlimited wealth", "I am the source of wealth", "I am money". Your paradigm will shift if you persist with working on wealth within.

The challenge and opportunity for you is to identify your definition for wealth. Your lifestyle as a wealthy person does not have to resemble celebrities who have huge homes, diamonds, and yachts. This is all fine, but you may yearn for a unique lifestyle. Wealth is freedom, freedom to choose what you want, how you wish to live.

Money is your friend. Treat it with the same respect that you would a dear friend. Change your relationship with money to one of appreciation.

Live long and prosper!

23

Move Your Body

This is a terrific tool I recommend to clients and friends in dealing with stress and depression. Keep moving. Exercise. Be outside in natural surroundings. Go for long hikes.

There are periods when you are between things, be it relationships or jobs. You are "in the void". Nothing is happening. You feel powerless. Equally stressful are times when you are overwhelmed, when you have created or life has given you multiple tasks and responsibilities and you feel you can not bear it one more nanosecond. Following your bliss seems like a joke. Not only can you not find or follow your bliss, you can not find where your house keys are. Bliss? It's like who moved my cheese. Who moved my bliss? Who moved my centeredness, my essence? You go through the motions, not feeling much.

Okay, you get the picture. I have been there. What I discovered is that keeping my body moving, getting out of the house or office to move my body outdoors or in the gym works wonders. I hit the trailhead with my mind a muddle, my body feeling like I weigh a ton, only to emerge in an hour or two feeling like I offloaded my baggage (of depressed and scattered thoughts).

When I was a psychotherapist, it was my practice to take clients on hikes in wild and beautiful places. One hike was to a volcanic crater in the middle of a forest on the Big Island. It was a mystical spot. The walk to the crater was about a mile. By the time we would arrive at what I called my office in the woods, the client would have begun to relax, become less depressed and be able to articulate their issues and feelings. It was absolutely amazing. This held true for teenagers, and with people who were non-verbal at the trailhead beginning the walk.

You may say you don't have the time. If that is your issue, I say make the time. Your health, centeredness and serenity require that you take the time to move your body.

This axiom is particularly useful when "in the void". When in this kind of state when nothing seems to be happening, it is important to take control of what is within your realm. Your body. Eat right and walk.

Energy blockages can occur suddenly or can be the result of accumulated stress and crisis. If you become aware of symptoms of burn out, such as waking up tired, having a "short fuse", not able to think clearly or transform your thoughts or feelings from the negative to the positive, you may be suffering from burnout and/or an energy blockage. I have found it helpful to redefine what I am experiencing such as redefining depression to anger turned inward or dammed up energy. It certainly feels that way to me when I have trouble focusing on beauty, goodness or hope. Everything is tied up inside. The remedy may be to get moving. Move my body even when initially I don't want to move at all. Just getting up and taking the steps to the door, to the car, turning on the ignition and getting to the beach or trail helps. I also take days when I don't drive at all and walk everywhere. Move your body. Get the oxygen and blood flowing. You are then releasing the energy that is blocked, enabling more joy into your awareness.

A friend went through a difficult time, sold all her belongings and hit the road. She traveled around the US then Mexico with all her belongings on her back. She remembered my talking about keeping moving during the "void" times when we had gone on a hike together when I was in one of these periods. She adopted this as her motto. "Move the body". She walked miles around and between Mexican villages. She found this to be therapeutic.

When I pull this card from the Follow Your Bliss deck, I ask myself if the message means to move my body to another location. Should I migrate? When doing readings and a client pulls this card (and they will pull it repeatedly if it is relevant), we explore if a move to another State or country or city would be beneficial.

Moving your body onto the trail or moving your life to another place frees up your energy and consequently, you are increasingly able to attract the good to you.

24

Notice Beauty All Around You

The morning I wrote this chapter, I harvested a rose from the bush behind my house. This is a plant that I put in a pot years ago. It rooted into the ground and produces fragrant, gorgeous roses all year round. As I cut it, the fragrance blew me away. I was in awe and appreciation for the gift of the rose.

Later, I hiked in a sacred area that is replete with the glory of Nature. The beauty of the place astounds me. Living in Hawaii, there is an abundance of magic and beauty. I have traveled internationally and found beauty everywhere. You can find beauty in a city, in art galleries, in the eyes of a child.

We are extraordinarily blessed on the Planet to be surrounded with innumerable flowers, plants, trees, animals, other species, sunsets, ruins of once great civilizations, rainbows, beautiful fabrics, foods, and people. I could go on and go.

My experience is that when I am aware of the magnificence around me, my soul is uplifted. My energy level increases, blocks dissolve, then I can begin the process of building energy to create what I want. I call this beauty therapy.

The trick is to notice what is around you, in your home, office, with your friends and family. Stop and smell the roses. Slow down.

Sunrise and sunset are times when we see the Earth in her most rhythmic, peaceful mode. Watch a sunset. Muse over the regularity of the sun's setting, the colors in the sky. I often think that God is an artist, so incredible are the blends of colors in the sky, the shapes of the clouds. Surely the Goddess is a cosmic painter.

Beauty can be found within yourself, within others, in relationships. When witnessing the purity and innocence of a baby, your vibration can be raised. The key is awareness, noticing, acknowledging the beauty.

Sit on a rock on a path in a forest. Be still, look around. Breathe deeply. This is aromatherapy from the natural source. Watch the birds, listen to birdsong. Once aware of the immensity of what is around you, turn within and see that immensity, that beauty inside you. Practice the same technique when around children. Find their innocence and purity within yourself. Surely it is there, like a lotus flower. We are all children, either lost or found in our world. Find yourself amidst the beauty around you.

If you live near a body of water, this is a super place to visit to be recharged. There are negative ions in the air which could explain why we feel refreshed by and in the ocean. Perhaps it is that we may have evolved from the ocean, lived our first nine months in a sea of sustaining fluid. Water has miraculous benefits to mind, body and soul. If you are not near a body of water, take a long bath, use aromic oils in the bath water. Soak. Meditate. Bless and thank the water for its healing balm.

Beauty is in the eye of the beholder. I imagine that you know what your sources of inspiration are and I may never have seen what you have seen or experienced. Wherever you receive inspiration from beauty, visit it often.

25

One Step At A Time/One Day At A Time

One of my favorite walks in Kona is a walk of a few miles beginning at 800 feet elevation down to sea level. There is a panoramic view of the ocean that is spectacular. I decided to do the walk this week, consciously taking it one step at a time. I covered the miles in record time, flying down the road. When I arrived at a shopping center, I bought a ticket to a movie, then waited and waited. There was a glitch with loading the film. The theatre manager came into the screening room and told us it would be a few more minutes to load the film. He gave us a choice of switching to another film if we wished. I chose to stay and used the time to meditate. I confess, I did have to contend with impatience when the few minutes lengthened into forty five minutes. I disciplined myself to continue to be still, look within, be there one moment at a time. Finally, the film started. It was wonderful. As I exited the theatre, the manager gave me two free tickets, and thanked me for dealing with the delay. It was all good.

Twelve step programs have a number of concepts or principles that recovering people are encouraged to incorporate into their lives. One day at a time is a basic principle. As I have been fortunate to work with recovering alcoholics/addicts and joined them at twelve step meetings, I have become familiar with these principles.

One day at a time, one step at a time.

Recovery from an addiction and a lifetime of sobriety is built one day at a time. If an alcoholic promises to never drink again as long as he/she lives, they are sabotaging themselves as they can not really envision or live sober with forever in mind. It has to be taken one day at a time. The alcoholic/addict can realistically state that they will remain sober today, sometimes taking it one hour at a time.

When you apply this wise principle to other aspects of your life, imagine how it will work for you. If you "bite off more than you can swallow", you will wind up with the proverbial stomach ache. It is similar to looking at a big chunk of apple pie. You put a whole piece in your mouth, swallow it without chewing. Okay, pass the heartburn pills. If you had taken a smaller piece, and eaten it one small piece at a time, you feel satisfied. It is wonderful!

When you embark on an ambitious project and feel overwhelmed at the scope, narrow your focus to the next logical step.

Looking at how you will manage finishing your Thesis or Doctorate, decide on the next simple task to be accomplished. That is manageable. One day, one manageable task at a time will take you to completion. You can release your anxiety so that you are immersed in that next small step, giving it your full creative energy.

Taking on what feels like an impossible responsibility all at once can bring on a frozen state of mind, physical symptoms that can be your body saying: "stop, I can't take this all at once". Becoming immobilized, having panic attacks, relapsing into drug use are possible results of trying to do too much or promising more than you can imagine delivering.

One step at a time, one day at a time.

Your journey to bliss is accomplished one step at a time. What is your first step? What can you do today that will bring you closer to realizing your dream? If it seems like an impossible dream, break it down into pieces that are possible. You have a dream of owning a beautiful home, have visualized the rooms, furnishings, the property. You may not have the money today to buy the house and furnishings, though you do have the money to buy something in the color scheme you have in mind. Or the pottery. Go for what you can comfortably do or have or be today and day by day, you will realize your dream.

26

Own Your Power, Own Your Life

"… Just by maintaining silence—not leaning, not pushing, not yearning—and controlling your emotional reactions, you dominate your psychology. You act out a silent strength even though you may not be resonating it deeply within as yet.
Don't give yourself away. Work quietly on your weaknesses, develop a reserve and mystery, be organized and self-sufficient, and keep your life to yourself. Knowledge is power. The knowledge you never speak of is silent power."
Stuart Wilde in *The Three Keys to Self-Empowerment*

This is major, friends. Empowerment. Personal power. I will share with you what I have learned about becoming empowered. To begin, here is my story of a major catalyst for empowerment from my life.

I was twenty seven. I had been running a slight fever and had pain for a few months. My physician sent me to the hospital for a biopsy when antibiotics and other treatments didn't help. I was sent home with a clean bill of health and a sense of great relief. Two days later I received a phone call from the physician's receptionist asking me in a very serious tone of voice to come in to see the doctor and to bring my parents. This naturally set off alarm bells in my head. My parents maintained their composure though we were all very, very nervous.

The doctor told us that two pathologists had looked over the biopsy results and had different opinions about whether there was a malignancy.

Another meeting was arranged with one of the pathologists present, my parents and I. We met in a huge conference room at a major hospital and sat around a large mahogany table. Time stood still and I recall everything happening in slow motion as the people I considered being the final authority on what was happening in my body told me that they didn't know what was going on, that it could be terminal cancer or nothing, and that they could not agree on a diagnosis, that these things "sometimes happen". Doctors as Gods, as final authorities about my body died for me in that hour.

I was given total control to decide to have major surgery or not. The surgery would be exploratory in nature or could mean the removal of major organs. It was my choice. I chose surgery.

The next pivotal event and remarkably clear memory is after I had been prepared for surgery, I became very sleepy from the medication. A nurse came and said it was time to go to the surgery room. I was put on a stretcher and wheeled down the long hall while in a twilight zone consciousness. My mother walked down the hall holding my hand not knowing if I would live or die or what was going to happen. When my mother was told to let go of my hand, I went into emotional crisis. Time stood still again and I knew I was alone with God. It was between my Higher Power and I as to what would happen now. Even though the physician who was to perform the surgery was a kind and competent physician (and this was reassuring), I had come to the realization that my Higher Power and I were at least on equal ground in determining the outcome of the surgery. I had prepared myself with prayer, solitude, eating right and then a complete surrender to my innermost being.

When the doctor came into the room after the surgery to tell my parents and I that I was fine, no malignancy had been found, it was anti-climatic for me. I knew it was up to me and my relationship with the Universe to remain healthy.

When I was released from the hospital, I went straight to a health food store and began the journey of self-care, exploration of alternative medicine and eating right that has continued to this day. I took the reins of my health and body. Though the experience was one of emotional and physical crisis and involved a mental shock to me, it brought about my greatest growth and empowerment.

Here are my thoughts and recommendations about becoming empowered:

- When confronted with negativity in the form of another's words, or an emotional barrage (or baggage), hold your tongue. Count to ten. Sleep on it. Be as non-reactive as you are capable of at that moment. Come back to the person or situation, if you so desire, when you are calm.

- Walk away from arguments, violence and threats.

- Choose for yourself what feels right. You are the final authority in your life. This includes sorting through what you are reading in this book. If someone gives you advice and it doesn't feel right, do not follow it.

- Experience is your greatest teacher.

- Doctors, teachers, partners, lovers, family, friends, therapists, politicians, everyone out there is trying to tell you how to live your life and what is right or wrong for you and with you. They are consultants to you, not authorities that know the absolute truth about you. Outside definitions and diagnosis are guides, not absolutes.

- Define for yourself what wealth is, what you want, and develop the self-confidence to design your own plan to reach financial goals. There are various tools and theories out there that are guides to achieving wealth. Combine these tools and theories with your own intuition and intelligence.

- Self-reliance and independence can be learned, self-taught. Think twice about having someone else do for you what you are capable of doing for yourself.

- A wise person once said: "Rules are meant to be broken." I am not saying that you should embark on a life of crime and lawlessness. Laws and rules change with time, so be aware that they can be temporary and transitory. I got a ticket once for making an illegal left turn. I complained to authorities that the law was wrong, that it was dangerous to have to make the turn where it was indicated. Within six months, the traffic lane changed and it was then legal to turn left where I had previously.

- You are a sovereign being. Meditate on what that might mean.

- You have total control over what you put into your body and mind. Exercise that control and freedom.

- If you tend to feel like a victim and blame others for your victimization, look at how you co-create these situations and what you gain from the one down position. How can you avoid a similar situation in the future? Forgiveness takes time, yet it is very healing if you can forgive the person who you feel wronged you. You are then coming from your inner strength, compassion and wisdom. Remember Gandhi and his use of non-violent resistance in the midst of oppression and injustice.

- Practice detachment. Your need for security and absolute knowing brings attachments, which can then make it difficult to pull away from a person, place, thing, or belief that may be harming you.

- You are a magnet. You become magnetized when you build a reservoir of energy within yourself. Building your energy is an important aspect of becoming free and manifesting what you what. (Remember the archer, being still, building her energy, concentrating on the target). To accomplish this, I recommend: 1. Spend time alone, disconnected from outside influences, including turning off phones and computers. Stay in the silence for whatever period you are comfortable. 2. Keep your goals and intentions to yourself as when you speak of them, you are releasing and losing the energy you need to build your energy to become magnetized.

- If it is congruent with your belief system, find a spiritual practice that will help you center yourself and feel inner peace. Yoga is one I recommend, though again, it has to feel right to you. Playing soothing music or walking in a natural setting can be utilized as spiritual practice. The idea here is to disconnect from externals, find something that helps you relax and focus within.

- You can change your mind, shift directions, start over. You are free. You own your life.

27

Pamper Yourself

Take yourself out on a date. Indulge in chocolate ice cream, chocolate anything. Go to the movies. Get a massage. Listen to your favorite music.

Love is a verb meaning to actively care for, in this case, yourself. Loving yourself is more than turning those loving feelings inward. Taking actions on behalf of yourself can and will increase your positive self-regard and confidence.

Here is a list of suggestions of ways to pamper yourself, to love yourself. It is not all inclusive. Add your own touch to the list.

- A motorcycle road trip anyone?

- Attend a concert

- Buy new clothing

- Consider an acupuncture treatment

- Eat at that restaurant you have been noticing and hearing about

- Explore Reiki

- Engage your lover in a day of mutual massage and love making, replete with candles

- Get a massage

- Go on a weekend outing at a fabulous locale

- Go camping, roast marshmallows by the fire

- Ice cream, ice cream, ice cream

- Plan, shop for and prepare a delicious meal

- Play a new video game

- Read a good book

- See an inspirational film or indulge in a movie marathon

- Soak in a long, warm bath

- Spend time in a sauna or a hot tub

- Surround yourself with flowers and plants

- Time for a hair cut, hair treatment, scalp massage?

- Try aromatherapy

- Visit a health sanctuary or a day spa

Pampering yourself means to indulge, spoil yourself. You deserve to be treated with incredible love, spoiled like a child. You are your own loving parent who wants to give yourself what you need.

You can lift yourself out of a funk. You are lovable.

28

Positive Affirmations

An affirmation is a statement you write or repeat to yourself that contains positive words that reverse negative programming. When you repeat these words, you are reprogramming yourself to hold life affirming beliefs about yourself and the Universe.

Examples of positive affirmations are:

- I am lovable

- I am wealth

- I am a money magnet

- I am a Child of the Universe

- My body expresses perfect health

- Nothing can stop my good from coming to me

- The ideal soul mate has come into my life

- There is only one power and presence in the Universe, in all my affairs, and that is God, the Good omnipotent

You can create your own affirmations, type them out in large, bold lettering and tape them next to your mirror, computer, in your bedroom. State the affirmations while you are driving, hiking, showering, or before you go to sleep. The repetition initially will seem monotonous. Trust that the affirmation is slowly impacting your subconscious mind so that your belief system changes into new, positive beliefs. As time goes by, you will likely discover you are emphasizing the words that move you and images will emerge. Memories of when good has come into your life in the form of new opportunities, interesting people, healing and prosperity will arise to further the conviction within you that the affirmation is the truth.

When I can touch the truth of an affirmation, it becomes real and I know without a doubt that what I want will come to me. The knowing, the conviction, the touching the truth of the basics of life brings peace, then a demonstration of the truth.

I combine the knowing, conviction and truth in my own affirmations in this manner: "I affirm with absolute certainty and conviction that I am one with the loving, abundant Universe and all its blessings and goodness flow to me easily." "I state with 100% certainty that the power and presence of God is all there is and pervades every area of my life."

I affirm that I am connected to you as you read these words and this connection is for both of our higher good.

29

Sexual Healing

We are sexual beings. We are sexual when we are babies or toddlers. When you discover your baby is exploring their body, you may be shocked. After the first time you see your little one exploring, you will hopefully come to realize that this is a natural stage in a human's development. The child feels no shame, only the joy of pleasure and discovery. The desire to explore their body and to experience pleasure is natural and beautiful. You witness sexuality coupled with innocence and purity.

As you grow and learn and begin to share your sexuality with others, experiences may occur that are less than beautiful. Sexual intimacy may be fine, though perhaps the other person rejects you afterwards, or does not love you or becomes abusive later in the relationship.

Our bodies are our first area of self-discovery, curiosity and self-esteem. If this prized territory is challenged or injured, even perceptually and not by actual harm, we can be wounded emotionally. I remember my first sexual experience which was with a boy I was in love with. Shortly after our initial foray into true sexual intimacy, he rejected me. The rejection precipitated years of feeling deeply vulnerable, angry and wounded. Sexual healing in the form of loving relationships first with myself, then with others was required to bring my self-esteem back. Therapy with excellent psychotherapists assisted me on my quest for healing. I also had to be honest with myself as to how

I helped create the break up in order to overcome the feelings of powerlessness.

Sexual healing can be a bumpy ride, fraught with ups and downs and with the joy of rediscovering oneself. I encourage you to consider massage, therapy, and celibacy for a period of time to clear your energy field.

If you choose to be celibate, experiment with reframing your view of the experience. Study the principles of tantra yoga. Building up your sexual energy for periods of time can lead to creativity, visions, and spiritual insight. As you hold your energy within yourself or are sexual only with yourself, you are able to see the past, present and future more clearly as you are not taking in another's energy. Along those lines, it is interesting to note that we exchange water vapor with others simply by being with them in a conversation, in their energy field. Think of what you are exchanging in the way of feelings, thoughts, fears, hopes, projections when you are as close to another human being as is possible during sexual intimacy.

The ability to hold and build your energy enables you to become a magnet to attract what you truly want to yourself. Reframe your thinking about celibacy from a difficult experience to one of growth.

On the other side of the coin, a good loving sexual relationship or even experience, if you choose the partner wisely, can go a long way to healing self-doubt and past traumas.

The key here is to understand that you deserve love and pleasure, that you are wired from birth to experience the heights of bliss and joy through intimacy without guilt or shame. I urge you to practice affirmations and visualizations about loving yourself and your body to bring your consciousness into the space where you will choose sexualove partners with wisdom and attract loving, conscious people into your life.

Here are examples of sexual healing affirmations:

• I deserve love

• I am innocent

- I deserve pleasure

- I am beautiful

- I attract the perfect sexualove partner who will honor and cherish my body

- I release all tension and suffering from the past that I have held in my body. My body and energy field are clear

As you affirm your beauty and right to pleasure, you will begin healing those wounds that have kept your sexual and loving energy constricted. When you are ready, you can and will find an echo of your self-love in another's gracious response to you.

30

Solitude

"It has been said that if you do not go within you go without"
David Cameron Gikandi in *A Happy Pocket Full of Money*

Those of us who treasure solitude deal with judgments from others. A person who craves solitude can be labeled as a "loner" or "anti-social". It could be that the criticisms of being a lover of solitude are self-criticisms.

I am one of those lovers of solitude. Being alone, totally alone, the only human in sight and within hearing range in a place of beauty is my kind of place. I often go out on long hikes where I can not hear another human voice, away from technology. It is here, in these "lonely", lovely habitats that I can hear my own soul. It is here in these isolated or wild places that Nature speaks to me.

Authors who cherished these places, such as Annie Dillard and Henry David Thoreau, spent periods of time alone in places of beauty. Dillard wrote *Pilgrim at Tinker Creek*, which won the Pulitzer Prize in 1974 and Thoreau wrote the classic *Walden*. The writer in me would love to spend time in a cabin in the woods reading and writing, allowing the natural sounds and smells to sooth my soul and fuel my creativity.

When you are worn down by external stressors, when depression haunts you, when you are overwhelmed by multitasking and the demands of twenty first century living, take a day in the country by yourself. Find the road "less traveled" and explore.

As you hike a trail that you love or one that you have never been on, you are not only taking in the beauty of the environment, you are giving your weary brain a rest. You might be able to hear yourself think. Only you. Not the expectations and demands of the outside world. Give yourself this gift of solitude to hear yourself, to feel yourself.

When I have a decision to make and am uncertain, I go out on these long hikes or sit on a rock and look at the ocean for long periods of time. It is during these reprieves of having to do, be or have something that I can truly hear and see what is my highest good. Nature will speak to me in the form of butterflies approaching me, dolphins dancing in front of me. I listen to the wind, to the trees as the leaves rustle, and to the surf. Through all these natural sounds, I hear, feel and see what is the next natural, organic step for me to take in my life. Just hearing these sounds is healing.

Solitude. Monks spend hours in solitude, in prayer. Brave souls venture out onto the ocean sailing alone, fly across the sea alone. They dare to go where people have not been before. In these challenging adventures in wilderness or unfamiliar territory, we find ourselves. We learn about our strengths and limitations. Our Spirits soar.

I have always thought that the Native Americans' tradition of vision questing was based on sound principles. Questing is what we are doing on the Planet. Looking for meaning, seeking our spiritual path. What better way to learn about yourself and your path than to experience Nature in the raw, to experience yourself, alone, in a place of beauty, even stark beauty.

I encourage you to defy the judgments within and without and take time to be by yourself. Unplug from all the gizmos and gadgets that beep, ring and fling electromagnetic signals and radiation at your brain. Chill out. Clean out. Commune with Nature. In the silence, you will hear yourself.

31

Speak The Truth

Have you ever been in a situation when you believed you saw the truth when others did not? It could have been watching friends argue and as an observer, you saw what was really going on underneath the anger. It could be that you are becoming increasingly frustrated with your girlfriend or wife who refuses to be sexually intimate as frequently as you wish. You believe she keeps you at a distance due to a history of abuse. A block stands in the way of increased intimacy. There may come a time when you choose to speak the truth as you see it.

The truth has a certain "ring" or vibration to it that moves a situation to the next level. In the case of your friends, you could mention to them that you have some thoughts on the anger you have seen them express toward each other. If they are open to your comments, you can proceed with something along these lines: "I have been listening to you and here is what I think is going on. I think you are not really upset about what you are arguing about. Couldn't this be about your fear of ... (whatever you think is underneath the anger)."

With your wife or girlfriend, you could say to her: "I love you and want to be closer to you and feel frustrated that you keep me at a distance. I think you push me away because of past hurts you have experienced. I am not the person who hurt you in the past."

I am a psychic and my earliest childhood experience of a clairvoyant nature was while on the floor looking up at my mother and her friend talking. I was looking back and forth at them, listening to their words, noticing their body language. I wanted to shout: "Why are you lying to each other?" They were talking but their words were empty. I could see underneath the words to the music of their hearts and souls. My passion for honesty and truth was born at that moment.

Timing is important when speaking the truth. When you feel like you are clear about what you are seeing and feeling, it is good to speak then, before you become explosive or implode.

In the workplace, we are encouraged to be quiet about what we know is going on, especially if there are issues of integrity and dishonesty or oppression. Much is at stake at the workplace. What we say and do effects our finances and security. What a great stage to play out our fear vs. integrity issues. I have many times spoken out to correct injustices, refusing to cower before an unreasonable supervisor. While these have been challenging events, I have often felt liberated when speaking the truth about how I have felt about mistreatment at the workplace or unfair conditions. I know this is not everyone's cup of tea.

The question is does the truth really set you free? It could be telling your spouse that you want to acknowledge what you both have been feeling, that the relationship is stale or over. It could be telling your child that you know they are using drugs and it is time to deal with the issue, set limits and follow through. It could be you want to share with a friend that you are noticing that their belief in scarcity and doom and gloom is creating negative currents in their life. Telling the truth will free up your energy so you can move on or move closer to another. The situation will change due to the truth as you experience it being shared.

It could be time to share your feelings of love with another.

Another area of speaking the truth is when an inner truth emerges within yourself. It could be about who you are at a deep level, your purpose in life, your values and intentions, spiritual truths or your vision for a better life. You could hear your inner voice repeat key phrases to you that at first you do not acknowledge, that are initially a whisper. Over time, the still small voice within speaks louder. You have touched your own truth. You can share this with another or embrace it within yourself. The acceptance of an inner truth will free up your energy to express more of yourself, will move you forward to connect with what is right for you.

My recommendation is to share the deepest and highest truth you are aware of so that you can free up the energy that has been blocked by denial, avoidance and lies. If this is a deeply personal inner truth, allow this to move you into action to honor your own truth.

32

Think Out Of The Box

We have been programmed and socialized by parents, school, peers, the media, prevailing prejudices and religions to believe, behave and think within a normal range. Lifestyle choices are dictated by the commonly held beliefs and visions we have of an acceptable life. To step out of the expectations of our culture is a threatening experience initially.

When making decisions, we usually look at options that are provided us by culture and media. Tunnel vision is prevalent. Solving problems are handled similarly. Probable solutions emerge from the box that we have drawn in our heads, based on socialization and programming.

To step out of the box, to erase the box in our minds, is an act of radical freedom of thought. To think out of the box can occur spontaneously when having pondered a challenging problem for months or years or when in a crisis. Having exhausted possibilities for resolution, from out of the blue, a new idea comes to us, often in an image or a voice in our heads. The thought is creative and revolutionary.

Boxes that exist in your mind can be stereotypes, prejudices, acceptance of "scientific fact", religious dogma, and parental expectations. Remember that science is changing so fast that what was considered fact and truth fifty years ago has changed and continues to be revolutionized.

Examples of out of the box thinking are:

- Rosa Parks did not plan on sitting in the front of the bus that historic day in December, 1955. She got on the bus, was tired, and spontaneously decided she would sit in the front of the bus. She knew the segregation laws, was involved in the Civil Rights movement, yet, what happened that day that changed our culture was she stepped out of the box of the law and racial prejudice.

- Mary Baker Eddy lived in the 19th century when women could not vote, were generally barred from religious positions and the practice of medicine. Prompted by needing to find effective healing remedies for illnesses she was plagued with, she stepped out of all the boxes of her time to explore alternative healing which led to the her discovery and creation of the Christian Science movement.

- In our present time, the entertainer, Sacha Baron Cohen, evolved a new form of comedy after creating eccentric characters, then going out in public while in character. His outrageous character, Borat, may insult you, even horrify you, yet when realizing the originality of Cohen in creating Borat, it is difficult not to applaud and admire him (Cohen). I suspect he is someone who has not only has stepped out of the boxes of acceptable behavior and norms of the entertainment industry, he thinks without boxes, period.

It is said that the solution to a problem is not found at the same level as the problem. One has to discover the solution at a higher or deeper level or step outside of current boxes.

Let's take out the invisible eraser and practice eracism by removing those boxes from our minds. Worlds of possibility, inventions, creativity, joy and insight reside in the vast spaces beyond boxes. I will postulate here that we are in a time when the boxes we have lived in are collapsing in on us, as evidenced by hatred, violence, religious dogma leading to wars, environmental crises and paranoia. Those belief systems that we hold on to do not work anymore. They could be leading us to a dead end. It is time for us to think beyond existing paradigms and discover humane, life-affirming and utterly new forms of living and being.

Think beyond all the isms of sexism, racism, and ageism. Step out of the boxes that have programmed you into thinking: "I can't do that", "That isn't possible for me", or "That won't work for me".

You are a pioneer, with a genius inside your mind and soul. Release these potentials! Long live eracism!

33

Thought Is Creative

You have heard and read about creating your own reality and thinking positively. What is this about? How do you create your own reality?

This may be very basic to many readers, yet it deserves to be repeated. I like to review the steps to creating your reality. You start by thinking about what you want, engaging visualization, affirmations, to create the world you want inside of you, in your words and in your thinking. Thoughts create your reality. Thoughts combined with your imagination, beliefs, feelings and actions are the powerful fuel for the creative engine that exists within you, that is you. If you consider that the life you are leading today contains the things, the quality of relationships, the level of comfort with money that you thought about months ago, maybe years ago, you begin to realize that you are always creating the present and the future in your mind.

Here is the challenge. It takes disciple to control your thinking, to direct your thoughts. It is said that the mind is a "drunken monkey". That gives rise to the image of an out of control, agitated state of being. Try as I might, I am not able to control my thoughts one hundred percent of the time. I am better at this than I was ten years ago, yet it is an ongoing journey, to turn around negative thoughts and images, to contemplate the positive and joyous in my mind.

One way I have discovered of dealing with the runaway mind is to change a negative image that appears unbidden. Let's say I see a gun or have a fearful image of someone attacking me. I immediately change the image to flowers coming out of the gun as someone pulls the trigger. Like an artist painting on a canvas, I transform the fearful image into one of humor and beauty.

The understanding of how the mind creates reality has its base in scientific research into the effect of mind on experiments. It is known that the experimenter in a research project effects the outcome of the experiment. We can not be separated from our reality. Our thoughts, our expectations and beliefs shape what occurs, what manifests in our lives. We are entwined with the rest of the Universe. We live and think in a totally connected web of being so that what you think affects the rest of creation. It is empowering to recognize how you can truly reach out and touch someone or something.

In the early years of my spiritual seeking, I was taken aback by the power of my thoughts and tried too hard to control my mind. If I had one catastrophic thought, I would then load on self-criticism. Tried as I might, I could not totally tame my thinking habits. In some of the reading I engaged in, the seeker was advised to think positively all the time to become the master of their lives and fate. Being mastery was an appealing prospect, I tried harder. I pushed myself too hard. If you can do this, control your thoughts one hundred percent, I salute and admire you. I am currently at the stage of accepting that I have a wide range of feelings and thoughts and aim to turn around negative thoughts and trends to the positive often. I have discovered that being paranoid about the effects of a negative thought is counter-productive. I am working on turning around one thought or trend of thinking at a time. I like to believe that the Universe recognizes my deepest and highest positive intentions and will act on those intentions to create from original Substance what I want and need.

I advise being gentle though persistent as you explore the power of your thoughts.

34

Trust Your Intuition

"One important step to hear and follow your intuition is simply to practice 'checking in' regularly. At least twice a day, and much more often, if possible (once an hour is great), take a moment or two (or longer, if you can) to relax and listen to your gut feelings."
From the book *Living in the Light.* Copyright 1986 Revised Edition 1998 by Shakti Gawain and Laurel King. Reprinted with permission of New World Library, Novato, CA. www.newworldlibrary.com

Our gut instincts are often right on. I would bet you have had the experience of not listening to your gut reaction and regretting it later.

We are wired with intuition. Intuition could be a carryover from the time in human history when we were vulnerable, lived in caves and had to rely on ourselves, our quick reactions to ward off danger or to head in the right direction to find food and adequate shelter.

As our brains developed, we came to rely on rational thinking and technology. Science evolved into a cause and effect, materialistic paradigm. This is all changing now. Intuition is gaining ground again as a reliable human faculty. Let's not forget that we have these reflexes, an inner knowing of what is right, what is best for us in our bodies.

Intuition is not rational, it is not based on science. It is your inner guide that asserts yes or no, go or stop, hold em or fold um (as the song says).

Your intuition may be telling you to go in an unknown direction that you sense will be a profitable opportunity, a growth experience. You gut may disagree with professional advisors and friends. Who and what do you trust?

I knew a man who had an uncanny reflex in the palm of his hand when there was money coming his way, when a financial opportunity would be profitable. His palms itched. This response was infallible. Through a period of trial and error, he came to respect his body's reaction. He must be a very rich man today.

The difference between intuitive hunches and psychic information is that psychic "hits" usually are accompanied by images (clairvoyance) or images with sound (clairaudience). Hunches may be the precursor to the full blow psychic experience.

Many years ago, when my children were young, about five and seven, we were at the beach in California. I had an experience that began as a hunch, but quickly evolved into a life saving psychic experience. We were almost alone on the beach, the girls were playing near me. I was gazing at the water when suddenly, I had a prickly feeling on the back of my neck. I felt that someone was staring at me. I became very anxious, my gut reaction was to grab my children and run. I fought the intuitive response initially which then developed into an unpleasant image (clairvoyance) and then clairaudience as a voice accompanying the image commanded that I should not turn around to see who was there, that we should go to the car. I acted. I stood up, told the girls to calmly get their toys and walk with me quickly to the car. Oddly, they didn't object. We walked at a brisk pace to the car which was parked at a higher elevation and had a good view of the whole beach, even the area behind where we had been sitting. Once in the car and looking down at the beach, I saw a man crouched behind a rotting log, looking out and scanning the beach. The prickly feeling occurred again on my neck. The next day, the headlines of the newspaper were that a man had killed a person at the beach near where we had been. A senseless act. I never doubted my intuition or psychic promptings again.

Intuition is a life saving innate tool you have. Trust your intuition, trust yourself.

35

Wait For A Clear Sign

As you are alert to signs concerning a decision you wish to make, be open to the information coming to you from unusual channels. I've had auto license plates have significant messages for me that were hard to ignore even though I tried to dismiss them. Another channel that a sign or signal can emanate from is a friend or co-worker. You are thinking about what to do about the relationship, when, out of nowhere, your co-worker initiates a conversation that has a message in it for you.

Let's go back to territory we have covered thus far. Everything is energy. We are connected in a Universal web of energy, at the sub-atomic level. Thoughts are creative. Believe. Ask for guidance. Trust your intuition. Putting this together, it seems to me that when your thoughts are predominately on the two or three paths you can take, on the decision you need to make, and you are asking for guidance about this subject, you will attract the information you need. An affirmation I state when I am in a dilemma is "everything speaks to me today".

Waiting till you have the sign you need, coupled with the intuition and energy within yourself that tells you what is right for you may take time. You can try to "push the river" and make a decision before you have clarity. When this occurs, trust that if what you have decided is not in alignment with your higher good, it will eventually fall away. You will have another chance to consider options. I have had the experience of choosing the lesser of two options, not following my dreams and hopes, to find that I can make the best of that decision. When I feel ready, I move forward.

The caution I would say about not following your dreams, is if you choose to stay in an abusive relationship or another self-destructive pattern is dictating your decisions, then you are obviously hurting yourself.

I believe that you will awaken to your beauty one day and leave those patterns behind, perhaps consulting with mental health professionals. The fact that you are reading this book tells me that the days of languishing in painful, abusive relationships and jobs is coming to a close for you. Bliss is a far cry from being battered, victimized or treated with disrespect. I presume you want to feel good.

So when looking at your options for the next step in your life, be loving toward yourself, aware of your dreams and your bliss and look for signs and messages from the Universe. You will be guided by these outer messages and your inner self. When these two come together, you know what to do. If you don't, it's still okay.

It's all good.

36

Visualize Your Highest Ideals

"Imagination is the ability to create an idea, a mental picture, or a feeling sense of something. In creative visualization you use your imagination to create a clear image, idea, or feeling of something you wish to manifest. Then you continue to focus on the idea, feeling, or picture regularly, giving it positive energy until it becomes objective reality ... in other words, until you actually achieve what you have been imagining."
From the book *Creative Visualizations*. Copyright 2002 Shakti Gawain. Reprinted with permission of New World Library, Novato, CA. www.newworldlibrary.com

We are going to take a journey to your big dream, your passion, the highest and best life you can imagine. I'd like for you to get comfortable, preferably lie down or sit under a tree in a place where you have solitude. Turn off the phones.

As you are getting comfortable and ready for this visualization, pay attention to thoughts and images you have about your big dream, what you want. You will take these spontaneous thoughts with you on this journey.

If you have quiet, soothing music you can play softly in the background that may help you go into a deep state, put it on now.

Close you eyes. Take a few deep breaths. I want you to imagine in your mind's eye that you have been told by a trusted friend that there is an amazing sacred site, an ancient city that can be found at the end of a lovely hike through a rainforest. The trail is marked and you will be going on it alone. Your friend tells you that when you reach the city, an amazing teacher will greet you and give you a tour of the site. You will know the teacher by his/her eyes and the purple robe they will be wearing.

You decide to take the journey and drive to the trailhead. You can visualize that you are in Central America where there are fabulous pyramid cities such as Tikal or you can visualize being in any dense forest or rainforest that you know of that raises your vibration.

You see yourself get out of the car, hike to the trailhead and begin walking. Take a moment to center yourself. Bring up those spontaneous thoughts and visions of what you deeply want for yourself. Follow your energy to what makes you feel blissful as you walk on the path to the sacred city.

If you have a number of ideas that float through your mind, that is good. Note the objections that arise, be aware of the "I can't", "it'll never happen", "it's out of my range" kind of thoughts.

Use all your senses to bring the environment alive for you. Smell the flowers, the rain from the morning, feel the slight breeze, marvel at the colors of the rainforest, hear the birds singing to you.

As you lose yourself in the meditation and on the path, you will suddenly emerge into a clearing. You see buildings, pyramid structures, some overgrown with vines. The site is dazzling. Then you see her/him. He beckons you with his hand to come to him. The purple robe she is wearing is of a light material you have never seen before. It shimmers. You approach the teacher and as you make eye contact, you feel something awaken inside yourself.

The teacher motions to you to follow her into the library. You do so without understanding that the pyramid structure is, in fact, a library of the Universe. Inside, it is larger than you could have realized from outside. The teacher motions for you to stand still as he/she approaches the stacks of thousands of books, somehow in perfect condition, untouched by Nature or time. He/she turns to you one more time for a quiet glance, then picks up a large book saying: "It's this one".

The teacher approaches you and advises you to think about your highest ideals, what you want most in life, to visualize the choices you have or want to have before you. After you have done so, the teacher hands you the book, telling you to open to the page that feels right for you.

Though you are hesitant, eventually you open the book and the pages seem to dance to the page that is meant for you to look at. There it is. Your name is in large, bold letters at the top of the page. The picture and words of your highest hope at this present time, the images of what you will manifest are there on the page. Take in the picture. Memorize it. The words on the page tell a story, your story of how you came to attract this wonder, this bliss to yourself. The story makes it abundantly clear that this good is seeking you, that there are beneficial forces in your world and out of this world that are conspiring to help you bring this vision into your reality. Let the words and images leap from the page into your consciousness and imprint themselves within you. You are given advice on how to transform your self-doubts and fears into hope. There are affirmations you can use to reprogram yourself so that the inner you, your divinity, is set free and able to move freely to create what you want.

Your highest ideals, your dream is now clear. It is yours to create, to claim and live.

As you open your eyes and come out of the meditation, take a few moments to relive the experience, remembering the sights, sounds, colors, images and the essence of your dream.

When you are ready, commit the experience to paper. In future days, when you are alone and quiet, relive the visualization. Consider creating a treasure map of your highest good that is right now moving closer to you.

It is alive.

Afterword

It is with sadness that I finish Bliss 101. During the process of writing the book, I have been blessed with days of joy and bliss practicing the basics. Throughout the experience, I have been able to move my energy out of the doldrums, beyond depression and through impasses. I have proved to myself the value of the information I have shared with you. You will decide the value of Bliss 101 for yourself.

Notable for me has been the exquisite experience of having the words flow. From the time I first heard "write the bliss book" after *asking for guidance*, I have not experienced writer's block. Never. Though I may have stalled in an emotional impasse about other issues, never about the book. In the back of my mind and in *dreamtime*, I have been formulating the body of material to share with you no matter what my mood has been.

Writing certain chapters, for instance, the chapter about energy, has been extremely rewarding. Keeping energy moving, seeing how energy is everywhere and connects us to each other and to what we intend to create has become critical to my understanding of life. Contained within this pocket guide to bliss and freedom are gems of action-oriented ideas on how to remove energy blocks. *Everything is energy* and *it's all good*.

An image that has persisted is that of an archer, poised with the bow taut, arrow aimed at the target. The bulls eye represents the dream, your bliss. The arrow is your energy about to be released. The archer is the vehicle (you), the instrument that guides the arrow (energy) to hit the target. *Be one-pointed* in living your dream, in connecting with your bliss in the same manner that the archer focuses on hitting the target.

The references to being a sculptor loomed large in my mind while writing *leave everything behind* and *let go*. I could see a sculptor carving an image from clay, shaving away (letting go) what was extraneous. The creative endeavor of bringing to form your inner vision requires the use of a scalpel or tool to remove what is covering the vision that lives within you.

A theme I discovered was the Garden of Eden, which became predominant while writing *earth first*. The premise that we live in a Paradise and don't know it, don't see it, don't nourish it kept appearing to me. We live on a fabulous, rich, abundant Planet with the ingredients of the Garden of Eden. I hope you explore this possibility with openness.

Writing the chapters on *owning your power and your life* and *think out of the box* had special meaning for me and charged my batteries. I became keenly aware of the boxes I have drawn around my actions and how these boxes constrict me. Erasing these boxes has enabled me to stretch and breathe easier. I believe standing outside of the boxes created by stereotypes is a master key in your finding bliss and freedom (eracism).

Each chapter tied in together and seemed to me to be a pocket guide on how to become empowered, a back to basics guide on creating your own reality with a new twist. *Visualize your highest ideals.*

I hope you have experienced a significant energy boost reading this guide and applying the tools contained within. Stay on the journey, never give up on yourself or your passions.

About the Author

Over the last 30 years, I have counseled and provided education as a therapist, consultant and psychic to thousands of individuals, couples, families and children.

Midway through my career in the mental health field, I recognized that within each person is a sound and wise sage. Even when we are not cognizant of our inner sage, she is there.

I have been creative most of my adult life, the creativity taking many forms and outlets. I have written three screenplays in the genre of spiritual cinema and science fiction. Bliss 101 is the second inspirational book I have written. I am involved with photography, being the manager of an online store on Oahu (Global Creations Interiors in Haleiwa, owned by Helen Zeldes-Collison) and provided the principal photography for the website: www.globalcreationsinteriors.com.

I spend much of my leisure time outdoors enjoying the beauty around me.

Resources

www.abraham-hicks.com
www.alcoholics-anonymous.org/BIGBOOKONLINE
www.blossomgreen.com
Cockell, Jenny. *Across Time And Death, A Mother's Search For Her Past Life Children*, Simon and Shuster, 1994. (You can order from amazon.com)
Dillard, Annie. *Pilgrim At Tinker's Creek*, Harper Magazine Press, New York, 1974.
www.everydayactivist.com
(everyday steps for everyday people to save the earth)
www.goodnewsnetwork.org
Griscom, Chris. *Ecstasy is a New Frequency, Teachings From The Light Institute*, (you can order book from www.lightinstitute.com).
Hicks, Esther and Jerry. *Ask And It Is Given*, Hay House, Inc, California, 2004
Holmes, Ernest. *Science Of Mind*, Jeremy P. Tarcher/Putnam, a member of PENGUIN PUTNAM Inc., New York, 1938, 1966, 1997.
www.imagesofone.com/comersus/digitalGoods/eBooks/Sampler-AHappyPocketFullofMoney.pdf
(free e-book sampler of David Cameron Gikandi's book; you can order the book from www.completeguidetomakingmoney.com)
www.marybakereddylibrary.org
www.nimh.nih.gov/

(this is the National Institute of Mental Health's site which has a wealth of information about mental health and can help you locate mental health clinics and practitioners in your area)

Thoreau, Henry David. *Walden*, A Fully Annotated Edition (Jeffrey S. Cramer, Editor), Yale University, 2004.

Rolling Stone Magazine, November, 2006, The Real Borat Finally Speaks, article on Sacha Baron Cohen by Neil Strauss.

www.time.com/time/time100/heroes/profile/parks01.html

(article on Rosa Parks by Rita Dove)

www.tut.com

(Totally Unique Thoughts)

www.wikipedia.com

(free Internet encyclopedia)

References

Gawain, Shakti. *Creative Visualization*, Nataraj Publishing, A Division of New World Library, California, 1978, 1995, 2002.

Gawain, Shakti and Laurel King. *Living in the Light, A Guide to Personal and Planetary Transformation*, New World Library, California, 1986.

Gikandi Cameron, David. *A Happy Pocket Full Of Money*, 2005

Griscom, Chris (with Wulfing Von Rohr). *Time is an Illusion*, Fireside Publishing, New York, 1986.

Hicks, Esther. *The Teachings of Abraham,* from The Secret DVD, produced by Rhonda Byrne, Prime Time Productions.

Holmes, Ernest. *The Art of Life*, Jeremy P. Tarcher/Putnam, a member of Penguin Group, New York, 1948.

Wilde, Stuart. *The Three Keys To Self-Empowerment*, Hay House, Inc., Carlsbad, California, 2004.

www.scienceofgettingrich.net.

(free download of Wallace Wattle's e-book: *Science of Getting Rich*; SOGR discussion groups; Rebecca Fine's Practical Genius [TM] Online Course).

Recommended Viewing

A Beautiful Mind
Conversations with God
Ghandi
Ghost
Pay It Forward
Peaceful Warrior
The Secret
What The Bleep Do We Know

On Your Computer

www.InnerGuidanceMovie.com
(free)

Share Your Empowerment Experiences

I am interested in defining moments in your life that have been instrumental in your becoming empowered and free. Your story may appear in a future book on the subject of empowerment.

You can mail your story to me via email or snail mail. Be sure to include your name, snail and email addresses and phone number so I may contact you.

Carole Prism
PO Box 1094
Haleiwa, HI 96712
__caroleprism@gmail.com__
__www.caroleprism.com__

978-0-595-45221-7
0-595-45221-3

CPSIA information can be obtained
at www.ICGtesting.com
Printed in the USA
FSHW022311030119